DATE

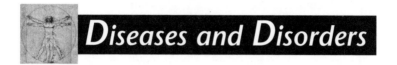

Schizophrenia

Titles in the Diseases and Disorders series include:

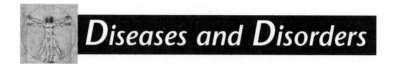

Schizophrenia

Titles in the Diseases and Disorders series include:

Diseases and Disorders

Schizophrenia

by Melissa Abramovitz

Library of Congress Cataloging-in-Publication Data

Abramovitz, Melissa, 1954–
  Schizophrenia / by Melissa Abramovitz.
    p. cm. — (Diseases and disorders)
Includes bibliographical references and index.
Summary: Discusses the nature of schizophrenia, its various types and diagnoses, and such related topics as Freud, genetics, family ties, stress, stigma, prenatal viruses, living conditions, daily problems, early treatments, funding, research, and new drugs.
  ISBN 1-56006-908-2 (hbk. : alk. paper)
  1. Schizophrenia—Juvenile literature. 2. Mental illness—Juvenile literature. [1. Schizophrenia. 2. Mental illness.]
I. Title. II. Diseases and disorders series
  RC514 .A245   2002
  616.89'82—dc21

2001002792

Copyright © 2002 by Lucent Books, Inc.
10911 Technology Place
San Diego, CA 92127
Printed in the U.S.A.

Table of Contents

"The Most Difficult Puzzles Ever Devised"

Cᴴᴬᴿʟᴇs Bᴇsᴛ, ᴏɴᴇ of the pioneers in the search for a cure for diabetes, once explained what it is about medical research that intrigued him so. "It's not just the gratification of knowing one is helping people," he confided, "although that probably is a more heroic and selfless motivation. Those feelings may enter in, but truly, what I find best is the feeling of going toe to toe with nature, of trying to solve the most difficult puzzles ever devised. The answers are there somewhere, those keys that will solve the puzzle and make the patient well. But how will those keys be found?"

Since the dawn of civilization, nothing has so puzzled people—and often frightened them, as well—as the onset of illness in a body or mind that had seemed healthy before. A seizure, the inability of a heart to pump, the sudden deterioration of muscle tone in a small child—being unable to reverse such conditions or even to understand why they occur was unspeakably frustrating to healers. Even before there were names for such conditions, even before they were understood at all, each was a reminder of how complex the human body was, and how vulnerable.

While our grappling with understanding diseases has been frustrating at times, it has also provided some of humankind's most heroic accomplishments. Alexander Fleming's accidental discovery in 1928 of a mold that could be turned into penicillin has resulted in the saving of untold millions of lives. The isolation of the enzyme insulin has reversed what was once a death sentence for anyone with diabetes. There have been great strides in combating conditions for which there is not yet a cure, too. Medicines can help AIDS patients live longer, diagnostic tools such as mammography and ultrasounds can help doctors find tumors while they are treatable, and laser surgery techniques have made the most intricate, minute operations routine.

This "toe-to-toe" competition with diseases and disorders is even more remarkable when seen in a historical continuum. An astonishing amount of progress has been made in a very short time. Just two hundred years ago, the existence of germs as a cause of some diseases was unknown. In fact, it was less than 150 years ago that a British surgeon named Joseph Lister had difficulty persuading his fellow doctors that washing their hands before delivering a baby might increase the chances of a healthy delivery (especially if they had just attended to a diseased patient)!

Each book in Lucent's *Diseases and Disorders* series explores a disease or disorder and the knowledge that has been accumulated (or discarded) by doctors through the years. Each book also examines the tools used for pinpointing a diagnosis, as well as the various means that are used to treat or cure a disease. Finally, new ideas are presented—techniques or medicines that may be on the horizon.

Frustration and disappointment are still part of medicine, for not every disease or condition can be cured or prevented. But the limitations of knowledge are being pushed outward constantly; the "most difficult puzzles ever devised" are finding challengers every day.

A Terrifying Disease

SCHIZOPHRENIA IS A serious mental disease that affects a person's thoughts, behavior, moods, and ability to work and relate to others. Although modern medicine can do much to help people with schizophrenia, it remains one of the most frightening diseases known to humankind. To an observer, the bizarre behaviors and speech of a schizophrenic are disturbing. For the schizophrenic, the world is a confusing maze of nightmares from which one cannot wake up.

Janice, for example, became schizophrenic during her adolescent years. To others she seemed "different," keeping to herself and avoiding social contact. To Janice herself, the strange thoughts and voices in her mind petrified her to the point that she refused to tell anyone about her problem. She was so frightened of being labeled insane that she banished herself to live in a distorted, isolated world.

In Janice's words, "The schizophrenic experience can be a terrifying journey through a world of madness no one can understand, particularly the person travelling through it. It is a journey through a world that is deranged, empty, and devoid of anchors to reality. You feel very much alone."[1]

The Personal and Social Toll

Even though doctors today can do much to help schizophrenics like Janice by using medications and other therapies, the disease is still not curable. As with other chronic disorders, patients and their families must make many adjustments to deal with schizophrenia on a day-to-day basis. This is emotionally, financially, and physically challenging for all involved. Emotionally, "all of a sudden

8

your hopes and dreams and goals change drastically,"[2] says mental health family advocate Janice Holmes. Medical insurance often does not cover all the costs of expensive medications and other therapy, so the patient's family must put out considerable sums of money. Finally, the demands of caring for a chronically ill person can be physically exhausting as well as time-consuming.

While some schizophrenia patients are able to work and live independently, many others require constant care and assistance and are not able to work. Many of these people live with relatives or caretakers; others are in mental hospitals or nursing homes. Still others are homeless and live on the streets or in homeless shelters. Experts in fact estimate that about one-third of the homeless adults in U.S. cities suffer from schizophrenia, making this mental disease a major social problem as well as a medical disorder.

The fact that 75 percent of all cases of schizophrenia begin between the ages of seventeen and twenty-five also contributes to the ongoing personal and social burden the disease creates. While most young adults are becoming independent, beginning careers, and otherwise taking their place as productive members of society, victims

Experts estimate that one-third of the adult homeless population in the United States suffers from schizophrenia.

of schizophrenia often find their family and career goals permanently shattered.

Unable to fend for themselves, many schizophrenics become dependent on the government for support in the form of Social Security or disability payments. The government also must often pay for medical care and related services like rehabilitation and psychotherapy when the individuals or their families do not have adequate health insurance. As a result, schizophrenia ends up costing taxpayers billions of dollars each year.

Adding to this social toll is the fact that many schizophrenics have a problem with drug abuse and tend to suffer from health problems associated with addiction. Doctors believe part of the reason for the

Unable to care for themselves, schizophrenics usually have to turn to family members or the government for help.

high rate of substance abuse is that drugs help the patient temporarily forget about having a chronic disease. Unfortunately, drug abuse can add to the mental confusion already present in a schizophrenic's brain. It can also lead to the same physical, mental, and social problems experienced by nonschizophrenic drug users.

Schizophrenics are also prone to early death from infections, heart disease, diabetes, breast cancer, and other illnesses. Experts say this may be partly because medical personnel are likely to ignore a schizophrenic's complaints, thinking that any reports of physical distress are imaginary and result from the person's mental malfunctions.

In addition to illness, suicide is another frequent cause of death among schizophrenics. Approximately 10 to 13 percent of people with the disease end up taking their own lives, usually as a result of being depressed about the prospect of living with an endless cycle of terror.

Experts now realize that helping schizophrenics lead productive lives does much to alleviate the financial and social burdens the disease creates. Doctors and government officials are beginning to work together to help schizophrenics learn skills that enable them to fit into a world which often pushes them aside because of the terrifying nature of the disease. These advances in addressing social and personal issues, along with ongoing research into improving treatments and fully understanding the causes of schizophrenia, have gone a long way toward helping people with the disease cope successfully and lead more fulfilling lives. Despite all these advances, for more than 2 million Americans, every day is a struggle with terror.

Chapter 1

What Is Schizophrenia?

PEOPLE WITH SCHIZOPHRENIA display a wide variety of symptoms and behaviors. Despite these diverse qualities, all schizophrenics share an inability to distinguish reality from fantasy. This characteristic is what unites the different forms and subtypes of schizophrenia into a single disease.

Doctors use the term "psychosis" to describe mental illnesses like schizophrenia, in which the person is incapable of separating what is real from what is imagined. People with psychotic disorders often cannot comprehend that they are mentally ill. To a schizophrenic, the voices he hears in his head or the demons he sees waiting to poison him are as real as the house he lives in. A schizophrenic patient named George expressed the overwhelming power of psychotic delusions (strong beliefs that have no basis in reality) very well when he explained that:

> The thing about delusions is that you totally believe them and nobody can convince you otherwise. It doesn't matter how strong a case they present. I can remember being in the hospital with one fellow who was convinced he was dead. The doctor asked him if dead men bleed and he said no, then the doctor poked him and he bled and the guy said, "What do you know, dead men do bleed!"[3]

Getting schizophrenics to recognize the fact that they are ill and need help is therefore one of the major challenges for doctors who treat this severe mental disorder. Moreover, doctors consider psychotic mental illnesses to be much more difficult to evaluate than the other type of mental illnesses called neuroses. While neuroses can be very serious, neurotic patients keep a firm grip on reality. This makes them more likely to understand the nature of their mental problem and to recognize that they actually have a problem.

Symptoms of Schizophrenia

Psychotic delusions are one of the most common symptoms of schizophrenia. They are an example of what psychiatrists refer to as positive symptoms. Other kinds of positive symptoms include hallucinations and inappropriate behaviors. Hallucinations involve a person seeing, hearing, or otherwise sensing things that are not really there. Many schizophrenics experience auditory hallucinations—that is, they hear voices which they believe are real.

Inappropriate behaviors take a variety of forms. Examples include laughing when informed that a tragedy has occurred, disrobing in

Hallucinations are one symptom of schizophrenia. Here, a brain undergoes a schizophrenic hallucination.

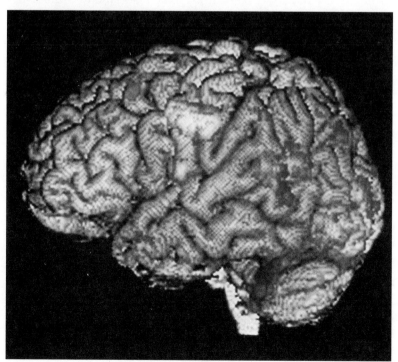

public or in front of strangers, and walking in circles or back and forth under a doorway. Other common behaviors are repeatedly shaking the head, grimacing, rolling the tongue, jerking the arms and legs, and stumbling and knocking things over.

Schizophrenics also display what are known as negative symptoms. Negative symptoms are the absence of behaviors and emotions present in normal people. Common negative symptoms include a lack of facial expressions, a refusal to make eye contact with others, and a lack of normal automatic movements such as blinking the eyes or swinging the arms when walking. Schizophrenics also frequently exhibit the negative symptom of not speaking or speaking very slowly. Many schizophrenics do not experience or display normal emotions like happiness and sadness. Doctors call this characteristic blunted emotions.

A third group of schizophrenic symptoms are called disorganized. As the name implies, these include incoherent, illogical, rapidly shifting speech and behavior. The most noticeable factor in disorganized symptoms is what doctors refer to as "loose associations"—unrelated thoughts and verbalizations the schizophrenic groups together. For example, a person with schizophrenia, when asked if he wants a cup of coffee, might reply that there are no cows in New York.

Subtypes of Schizophrenia

Such a wide variety of symptoms makes schizophrenia difficult to diagnose. Depending on the symptoms, a doctor classifies an individual as having one of a number of subtypes of schizophrenia.

Physicians have divided schizophrenia into several subtypes ever since the illness was first identified by the German psychiatrist Emil Kraepelin in 1893. Even before then, however, doctors wrote about a collection of symptoms they referred to as adolescent insanity or the insanity of pubescence. Patients with these symptoms were mostly teens and young adults who seemed disinterested in life, careless in grooming, incoherent in speech, and showed very erratic and disorganized behavior. Some patients ran around raving incoherently while others stayed stuck in rigid postures for hours or days on end. Many displayed no emotions or inappropriate emotions such as laughing at a tragedy. Many also had hallucinations and delusions.

Before Kraepelin's time, physicians divided these cases of adolescent insanity into three disorders. The first disorder, hebephrenia, applied to someone who had extremely disorganized thoughts and could not carry on a rational conversation. The second, catatonia, included patients who stayed unmoving in bizarre postures. The third, paranoia, categorized those who were obsessed that people or things were out to harm them.

Kraepelin, however, grouped these three types of adolescent insanity into a single disease he called dementia praecox, meaning that it affected a patient's ability to think (it made them demented) and tended to strike young people (praecox means early or precocious). He classified hebephrenia, catatonia, and paranoia as the three subtypes of dementia praecox, explaining that all three shared a common cause and a common prognosis.

Kraepelin believed the common factor that united these three subtypes was a physical deterioration of the brain. He believed this brain damage produced thought distortions along with a variety of odd behaviors including involuntary arm movements, strange tongue and eye movements, and tremors often seen in people with the disease. He also stated that this brain damage was responsible for the odd-shaped heads, low-set ears, thin lips, and unusually shaped fingers and toes he observed in many schizophrenics.

In Kraepelin's view, this brain deterioration made it unlikely that anyone with any of the three subtypes would ever recover. In his renowned textbook *Psychiatrie*, he wrote that patients with a "psychopathic disposition" for

German psychiatrist Emil Kraepelin was the first to say the three types of adolescent insanity were symptoms of one disease.

dementia praecox would not get better because the physical problems in their brains were irreversible. This, of course, made patients and their families dread receiving a diagnosis of dementia praecox, since the expert himself offered no hope for the future.

Dementia Praecox Gets a New Name

Although other doctors agreed that Kraepelin was correct in grouping hebephrenia, catatonia, and paranoia into a single disease, some did not share his view that people with dementia praecox suffered from brain damage. The Swiss psychiatrist Eugen Bleuler was one of the best-known experts to put forth the viewpoint that dementia praecox did not derive from a physical deterioration of the brain. He wrote extensively about his observations that some patients seemed to get better for no apparent reason, signifying that no permanent brain damage was present. Bleuler also found in his medical practice that the disorder did not always start early in life, so he believed Kraepelin's naming the disorder dementia praecox was also inappropriate.

Bleuler explained in his 1911 textbook that the central problem in the disease was a psychological "splitting" rather than a physical decaying of the brain. To describe this condition, Bleuler renamed the disease schizophrenia. The word "schism" means a split and "phrenic" means mind or brain. Unfortunately, many people have misinterpreted the term "schizophrenia" to mean a split personality, and this has led to confusion over the disease. Schizophrenia does not involve a split personality. The split Bleuler referred to was in the patient's reasoning capacity. When he wrote, "In every

Swiss psychiatrist Eugen Bleuler gave schizophrenia its name.

case we are confronted with a more or less clear-cut splitting of the psychic functions,"[4] Bleuler meant that someone suffering from the disorder could not use intellect to distinguish fact from fantasy. In his view, this confusion over what is real was indeed the quality that united the different subtypes Kraepelin had identified into a single disease.

The Modern Subtypes

In addition to giving schizophrenia its new name, Bleuler also added a fourth subtype called simple schizophrenia to Kraepelin's original three subtypes. Modern mental health experts continue to recognize these four subtypes, although they have reclassified hebephrenia as a disorganized subtype because of the preponderance of disorganized symptoms that define it. They have also given simple schizophrenia the new name of undifferentiated subtype since it involves symptoms commonly seen in the other subtypes. In addition, modern doctors have added a fifth subtype, residual subtype, to the description of schizophrenia. Residual subtype is characterized by residual, or leftover, symptoms after a patient has undergone successful treatment for the original symptoms.

Doctors today diagnose schizophrenics with one of these five subtypes depending on the symptoms they display. It is often difficult to diagnose a patient as having one particular subtype because many symptoms overlap and change over time. As a result, the patient's most prominent symptoms are used to determine the category that fits best.

Paranoid Subtype

Of the various subtypes, paranoid schizophrenia is the most common form. Paranoid schizophrenics typically experience delusions in the form of exaggerated fears that someone or something is out to do them harm. Steven, a college student, received a diagnosis of paranoid schizophrenia after he began eating food only directly from a can in the belief that other people were trying to poison his food. He also avoided girls on campus since he believed they would shoot poisoned spiderwebs at him which would entangle his body.

Paranoid schizophrenics typically believe that someone or something is out to harm them.

Many paranoid schizophrenics also believe that others can hear their thoughts. This tends to make them afraid that other people will retaliate if these thoughts are at all bizarre or threatening. Another typical belief is that the paranoid individual is on a special mission in life or that various objects have special meaning for them. For example, to a paranoid schizophrenic, a traffic light might be considered a signal from space aliens.

Catatonic Subtype

Catatonic schizophrenics also suffer from delusions, generally believing that they must remain motionless or focus exclusively on certain limited motions in order to avoid catastrophic consequences. This form of schizophrenia is characterized by the patients' grossly abnormal motions or lack of motion. Many catatonic schizophrenics lock themselves into rigid postures for hours or days at a time. One catatonic woman in her early twenties sat curled up, unmoving and silent for days on end because she believed, "if I spoke, the air around my very universe would shatter . . . if I moved, I would bring disaster to the world."[5]

Catatonic schizophrenics who remain immobile must often be fed by force and typically do not unfreeze themselves even to use the bathroom. If someone else moves one of their limbs, it remains motionless in the new position, a characteristic doctors call "waxy flexibility." Some catatonics keep repeating motions—known as echopraxia—or sounds—known as echolalia. Others alternate between immobility and frantic activity.

Undifferentiated Subtype

People with undifferentiated schizophrenia display varied symptoms found in the other subtypes of schizophrenia. Doctors diagnose a patient with undifferentiated subtype when none of the symptoms stands out enough to warrant categorizing the person as a paranoid, catatonic, or disorganized schizophrenic. Rick, for instance, suddenly vanished. His family found him in a nearby town

Catatonic schizophrenics may stay motionless in strange positions for hours or days at a time.

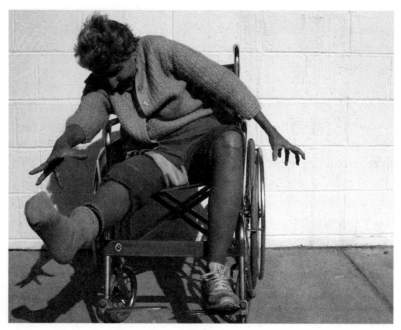

and took him to a hospital, where he claimed he was Jesus Christ and could move mountains. His speech was incoherent as he ranted on that his food was full of ground-up corpses; at other times he spoke in a more understandable fashion. Since he showed symptoms of both the paranoid and disorganized subtypes, he was diagnosed with undifferentiated subtype.

Disorganized Subtype

The most prominent symptom in the disorganized subtype of schizophrenia is consistently incoherent speech and behavior. A conversation between a patient named Mary and her doctor is a clear example:

> Doctor: Can you tell me the name of this place?
>
> Mary: I have not been a drinker for 16 years. I am taking a mental rest after a icarter assignment or "quill." You know a "penwrap." I had contacts with Warner Bros. Studios and Eugene broke the phonograph records but Mike protested. I have been with the police department for 35 years. I am made of flesh and blood see doctor? (She pulls up her skirt).[6]

Disorganized schizophrenics are also likely to show inappropriate emotions and behaviors like giggling, smiling, and grimacing for no apparent reason.

Residual Subtype

A residual schizophrenic is someone who doctors consider to have been successfully treated for some type of schizophrenia, but who has some remaining, or residual, symptoms. Residual symptoms are usually negative symptoms. One patient with residual schizophrenia showed the typical negative symptoms of being very quiet, passive, and uninterested in what was going on around him. His face was expressionless and his doctor noticed that he did not seem to care about anything. During his therapy sessions the man was polite, but never happy or sad.

Despite being considered successfully treated, this patient continued to display decidedly abnormal behaviors. One day he set fire to

Schizophrenics, like this man, experience three different phases of the disease.

his own house, then sat and watched television until firefighters arrived and informed him the house was on fire. He got up, walked calmly outside, and watched the house burn without saying a word.

Phases of the Disease

In addition to the diagnostic difficulties posed by the various subtypes, doctors find the fact that the general course of the disease involves three phases complicates matters. The first phase is called the acute phase. It contains active symptoms which can include hallucinations, delusions, catatonia, disorganized thoughts, and negative symptoms. How long this phase lasts varies widely, from as little as a few hours to several years.

During the second phase, known as the stabilization phase, acute symptoms gradually decrease and the person regains the ability to function more or less normally. This phase may last six months or more, and after this the schizophrenic ideally reaches the third, or stable, phase of the disease, in which symptoms are absent or much less severe than in the acute phase.

Just as there are a diverse range of symptoms involved in the disease, wide variations also mark the course of each patient's progress. The majority of schizophrenics go through cycles in which they reenter the acute, stabilization, and stable phases for varying lengths of time. Some patients never get past the acute phase; others remain in the stable phase for years at a stretch.

Schizophrenics, like this woman who broke into the home of David Letterman, suffer from many symptoms, including hallucinations and delusions.

Difficulties in Diagnosis

Diagnosing schizophrenia is difficult not only because of the vast range of symptoms and their cycles, but also because the disease develops at a different rate in each patient. Most cases unfold gradually, progressing from a loss of interest in school or work, difficulty concentrating, sleep problems, and social withdrawal to hallucinations, delusions, and disorganized behavior. However, for some patients, the symptoms come on suddenly. In the early stages, some schizophrenics' symptoms may resemble other disorders such as depression. This period of milder symptoms, known as the prodromal period, can last for days, weeks, months, or even years.

Another factor which complicates diagnosis is that not all cases of schizophrenia begin between the typical ages of seventeen and twenty-five. Psychiatrists must be alert to the fact that older or younger individuals may also develop schizophrenia. There are rare instances of what doctors call late onset schizophrenia beginning after age forty and of childhood schizophrenia beginning before age fifteen. Since these types of schizophrenia are unusual, they tend to be mistaken for other forms of mental dysfunction.

The Schizophrenia Spectrum

Illnesses known to psychiatrists as "schizophrenia-spectrum" diseases share some of the characteristics of schizophrenia, making accurate diagnoses even more difficult. For example, one schizophrenia-spectrum disorder is schizoaffective disorder, which includes severe depression or manic mood episodes along with typical schizophrenic symptoms. Manic mood episodes are the opposite of depression. A person who is manic has unrelenting energy and frantically moves from one task to another. Schizophreniform disorder, the second schizophrenia-spectrum disease, is identical to schizophrenia except it lasts less than six months, and schizotypal personality disorder, the third, produces milder symptoms than schizophrenia. Sometimes people with schizophreniform disorder and schizotypal personality disorder take a turn for the worse and go on to develop full-blown schizophrenia; for this reason it is important for a doctor to closely monitor these conditions and adjust the patient's diagnosis and therapy if needed.

Before a psychiatrist can actually make a diagnosis of schizophrenia, first these related schizophrenia-spectrum disorders along with other conditions that can produce similar symptoms must be ruled out. Certain drugs, such as cocaine and amphetamines, can produce such symptoms. Tumors or lesions in certain areas of the brain may also cause a person to act schizophrenic. A doctor can rule out these diseases and drug-induced problems by taking a detailed medical history, performing a complete physical and psychological examination, and analyzing laboratory tests.

Making the Diagnosis

In the end, most psychiatrists base their diagnosis on both the length of time a patient has had symptoms and how severe these symptoms are. Psychiatrists refer to the fourth edition of the *Diagnostic and Statistical Manual of Psychiatry* (known as the *DSM-IV*) for guidance in making this determination. Basically, the

In order to make an accurate diagnosis of schizophrenia, doctors must perform a complete physical and psychological exam.

DSM-IV recommends a diagnosis of schizophrenia if the patient has some psychotic symptoms for at least six months, two or more active symptoms for at least one month, and an inability to interact with others or work productively.

Diagnosis in Other Cultures

As with any medical decision, the doctor's own judgment and experience also play a role in determining whether or not someone is diagnosed as schizophrenic. Sometimes, in fact, a diagnosis of schizophrenia has as much to do with the doctor's own culture as with some absolute standard.

The modern criteria for diagnosis apply primarily to the United States and other Western countries, although language differences can influence how experts view and therefore diagnose schizophrenia even in these regions of the world. According to researcher Vicki Ritts:

Language differences limit the equivalency of diagnosis between schizophrenia in the U.S. and Germany. For example, Gedankenentzug (literally "withdrawal of the capacity to think") is considered a basic symptom of schizophrenia by German psychiatrists. American and British textbooks, however, make no specific reference to it. Furthermore, patients who speak English do not report such symptoms.[7]

Also impacting diagnoses are cultural norms. While schizophrenia occurs throughout the world, various cultures tend to interpret its symptoms in different ways. In India, for example, doctors are less likely than in America to diagnose a person suffering from hallucinations and delusions as a schizophrenic. This is because, as Ritts notes, "In India some people [with hallucinations and delusions] are spirit mediums or avatars who permanently take on the role of a Hindu god. Thus, in the Indian view these persons are considered to be a human incarnation of a god and not suffering from schizophrenia."[8]

Cultural differences can, in addition, shape the expression of specific symptoms exhibited by people with the disease. In contrasting the types of symptoms typically seen in schizophrenics in Western countries and in India, Ritts notes that "Hallucinations in the West often reflect technological features of society while hallucinations in India are more likely to take the form of ghosts, spirits, or animals. Delusions also reflect the cultural beliefs and religious views."[9]

Another way in which cultural ideas affect the symptoms and diagnosis of schizophrenia is illustrated by studies of the disease in Japan. Even when Japanese patients show severe catatonia or other classic symptoms of schizophrenia, doctors there are much less likely to diagnose the person as a schizophrenic due to a strong cultural aversion to doing anything that might reflect negatively on the patient's family. In Japan this sense of shame is so profound that Japanese doctors are likely to diagnose a physical illness known as neurasthenia in someone who shows schizophrenic symptoms. By making such a diagnosis the doctor helps the family and the patient avoid the stigma of mental illness.

The Antipsychiatry Movement

Even in the absence of linguistic and cultural differences, whether someone is diagnosed as schizophrenic sometimes depends on the philosophy of his or her doctor. For example, in the 1960s a group of experts and laypeople introduced the "antipsychiatry movement." Supporters of the movement believed that schizophrenia and other mental illnesses resulted from social, political, and legal definitions rather than biology and environment. Proponents said schizophrenia was a nondisease, or myth, created by social definitions of insanity.

Experts such as sociologist Ervin Goffman, and psychoanalyst Thomas Szasz, in his book *The Myth of Mental Illness*, argued that the whole problem with mental patients was in how they were labeled

Books and movies like One Flew Over the Cuckoo's Nest *supported the antipsychiatry movement of the 1960s.*

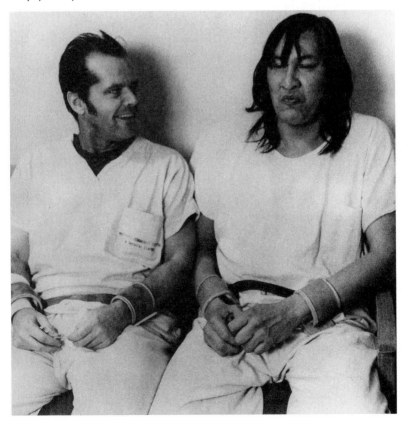

as "sick." British psychiatrist Ronald D. Laing, author of *The Divided Self*, went further, arguing that society, not the patient, is ill: "Schizophrenia is a rational response to a mad society. . . . Future generations will see that what we call 'schizophrenia' was one of the forms in which, often through quite ordinary people, the light began to break through the cracks in our all-too-closed minds."[10]

The general public also began to doubt the existence of mental illness following the publication of Ken Kesey's novel, *One Flew Over the Cuckoo's Nest* in 1962. Many people began believing the book's central idea that psychiatrists were simply creating mental illnesses in order to exercise their power to lock people up in mental hospitals.

While some experts continue to subscribe to the antipsychiatry viewpoint today, the consensus among doctors is that it is not a valid line of reasoning. Mounting evidence that schizophrenia and other serious mental illnesses are biological disorders with definable causes has convinced most people that these are real diseases rather than social or political labels.

Chapter 2

What Causes Schizophrenia?

E VER SINCE SCHIZOPHRENIA was first identified as a disease, experts have debated its causes. Some, like Emil Kraepelin, believed biological factors in the brain caused the disease. Others subscribed to Eugen Bleuler's view that schizophrenia resulted from psychological abnormalities. Still others held that social and environmental variables were responsible.

The best-known proponents of the social and environmental explanations were Viennese psychoanalyst Sigmund Freud and his followers. Freud believed that a person's unconscious memories of traumatic childhood events were the cause of schizophrenia. Other psychoanalysts expanded Freud's ideas to include other culprits besides unconscious memories. The well-known psychiatrist Harry Stack Sullivan, for example, believed that an individual's inability to deal with anxiety caused schizophrenia. In the 1930s psychoanalyst Dr. Freida Fromm-Reichmann published her views that a mother who was cold and distant could cause her children to develop schizophrenia. Fromm-Reichmann wrote, "The schizophrenic is painfully distrustful and resentful of other people due to the severe early ways and rejection he encountered in important people of his infancy and childhood, as a rule, mainly in a schizophrenogenic mother." [11]

In the 1940s, Dr. Theodore Lidz of Yale University expanded Fromm-Reichmann's theories to include entire "bad families" as causes of schizophrenia. But when researchers actually tested Lidz's and Fromm-Reichmann's ideas by employing controlled studies, the data showed no evidence that mothers, fathers, or other family members were direct causes of the disease. In fact, in most families in which one child is schizophrenic, other children are normal, so chances are the parenting practices have nothing to do with causing the disease.

A Combination of Causes

Eventually, scientific evidence that schizophrenia has strong biological roots convinced most experts that the causes of the disease were not environmental and were in fact quite complex. In the 1950s, psychiatrist Paul Meehl developed a theory that certain biological, environmental, and social factors interacted to produce the disorder. His theory, known as the diathesis-stressor model, describes three stages in the development of schizophrenia. In the first stage, an inborn defect results in a brain abnormality Meehl called schizotaxia. In the second stage, people with schizotaxia learn and think abnormally, resulting in a personality pattern he named schizotypy. During the third stage, certain environmental difficulties can trigger the development of schizophrenia in a schizotypal person. According to Meehl's model, all people born with schizotaxia go on to develop schizotypy, but not all end up with schizophrenia.

The Modern View

Most modern experts hold a similar view regarding the combined causes of schizophrenia. They believe that the primary cause is genetically determined biological abnormalities in the brain.

Sigmund Freud believed schizophrenia was caused by a person's unconscious memories of traumatic childhood events.

But some of these abnormal features may in turn be triggered into producing schizophrenia's symptoms by environmental and social stress factors such as a difficult birth, a viral infection, poverty, physical or emotional abuse, or even simply living in a crowded city. Different people may be affected to varying degrees by these biological, environmental, and social elements.

The more social and environmental stress factors there are, the more likely a biologically predisposed person is to become schizophrenic. Conversely, the effects of these stress factors can be offset with protective factors like being employed, having strong family ties and close friendships, and receiving good medical care for mental and physical problems. Many experts also believe these protective factors make a big difference in how well schizophrenia's symptoms can be controlled after they develop.

The interaction of social and environmental stress factors with biology is clear in the case of Dallas, who had a strong family history of schizophrenia. His great aunt, two uncles, father, and brother all showed signs of severe psychosis. Dallas was also physically and emotionally abused as a child by various family members who beat him and told him he was worthless and evil.

Dallas developed schizophrenia in his early twenties when he began experiencing hallucinations, delusions, and disorganized thoughts. Over the years many of his delusions involved torture and fear of torture. His therapists believe this resulted from actual events in his life interacting with a genetic predisposition to produce his particular brand of the disease.

The Case for a Genetic Cause

Extensive scientific research supports the viewpoint that a genetic predisposition is a primary factor in causing schizophrenia. A genetic predisposition is not the same thing as a directly inherited characteristic such as hair color, eye color, or skin color, since it is uncertain whether someone predisposed to a disease like schizophrenia actually will develop symptoms.

Doctors have suspected a hereditary element in schizophrenia ever since the disease was first identified. Emil Kraepelin, for example, noted that about 70 percent of his schizophrenic patients had

During the 1920s, scientists began studying twins to see if heredity played a part in schizophrenia.

family members who also suffered from the disease. Other doctors found similar clusters of schizophrenia in families.

Still, the question of whether heredity or merely common environmental factors caused multiple cases of schizophrenia within families led scientists in the 1920s to begin studies of twins and adopted children. Researchers reasoned that if genes were indeed responsible, genetically identical twins should both develop schizophrenia at a greater rate than nonidentical siblings did. These researchers also predicted that if identical twins raised in different adoptive homes both developed schizophrenia, this would be even more proof for the role of heredity.

One of the first researchers to systematically study schizophrenia in twins was Hans Luxenburger of Bavaria, Germany. Luxenburger found that both individuals in the identical twin pairs he studied developed schizophrenia 58 percent of the time. Subsequent studies have found similar results in the 50 to 60 percent range. The rate is about 15 percent for fraternal, or nonidentical twins, who do not have identical genes. In the general population, researchers find the rate to be about 1 percent.

Family Ties

Further research helped determine that heredity, rather than a common home environment, accounted for the high percentage of identical twins who both become schizophrenic. In 1959, Dr. Seymour Kety of the National Institute of Mental Health in Bethesda, Maryland, began a series of studies on children of schizophrenics who had been adopted or otherwise reared separately from their biological parents. Kety discovered that adopted children with schizophrenic biological parents were much more likely than those with nonschizophrenic biological parents to develop the disease themselves.

Other studies suggest that environment only comes into play when schizophrenia is already present in someone's biological family. Such investigations show that children whose biological parents are mentally healthy but whose adoptive parents are schizophrenic have only a 1 percent chance of developing the disease—the same chance as the general population. In contrast, studies show that people who have one schizophrenic biological parent have an 8 to 18 percent chance of getting the illness. With two schizophrenic parents the risk rises to about 46 percent. This indicates that people who have a greater chance of inheriting any genes related to schizophrenia also have a greater probability of developing the disorder.

Where Are the Schizophrenia Genes?

The fact that not everyone with a family history of schizophrenia develops the disease has also led scientists to surmise that more than one gene is involved. Several researchers have tried to pinpoint exactly which genes are responsible, but so far no one has made any definitive findings. Using genetic mapping techniques, one group of scientists found twelve chromosomes that are likely to carry genes related to schizophrenia, but the precise genes and locations have not been established.

Investigators hope that techniques like genetic mapping, which involve studying the genetic makeup of certain families with known inherited tendencies and then using computers to help locate the responsible genes on their chromosomes, will soon lead to a new understanding of the role of heredity in schizophrenia. In one study presently being conducted at the University of Utah, researchers are scanning several genes on chromosome 22 for mutations that might be related to the development of schizophrenia. As experts at the National Institute of Mental Health explain, "an arsenal of new molecular tools and modern statistical analysis are allowing researchers to close in on particular genes that might make people susceptible to schizophrenia by affecting, for example, brain development or neurotransmitter systems governing brain functioning."[12]

Schizophrenia Genes and the Brain

Besides trying to identify and locate the genes involved in schizophrenia, scientists are also doing a great deal of research to find out exactly how these genes cause the disease—for example, by determining structural abnormalities in the brain. Many studies, beginning with early research that relied on autopsies, have shown that the brains of people with schizophrenia are different than normal brains. Doctors in the early 1900s found during such autopsies that many schizophrenics had enlarged brain ventricles. These are the canals within the brain where the cerebrospinal fluid circulates.

Scientists have not yet been able to identify the genes involved in schizophrenia.

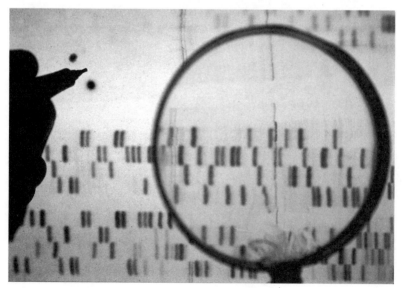

New techniques, such as MRI (magnetic resonance imaging), PET (positron emission tomography), and CT (computerized tomography), which allow the viewing of the brain in living people, confirm that enlarged ventricles are present in the brains of most schizophrenics. How this affects the symptoms or progress of the disease is as yet unknown, but research to try to find out and perhaps to use this knowledge as a diagnostic tool is continuing.

Common Structural Abnormalities

Researchers using MRI, PET, and CT scans have found structural abnormalities in various areas of the brain that control thinking, feeling, perception, coordination of mental processes, and movement. As the scientists study these structures, they learn more about how each correlates with specific symptoms seen in schizophrenia.

Some of the most common abnormalities among schizophrenics are decreased size in structures called the hippocampus and amygdala, located in the section at the base of the brain known as the lim-

A PET scan shows the difference between a normal brain and one affected by schizophrenia.

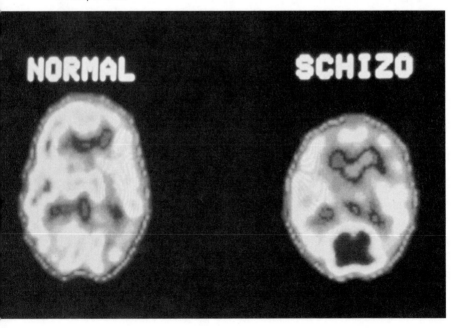

bic system. The hippocampus is important in the ability to learn, while the amygdala is crucial in controlling aggression and in sensory and emotion processing. Scientists have found that damage to these areas produces hallucinations, distorted sensations and perceptions, and inappropriate behaviors, so they suspect that somehow these abnormalities cause similar symptoms in schizophrenics. Further evidence that damage to the limbic system is linked to schizophrenia comes from medical observations that other brain disorders in this region, such as tumors or encephalitis, can cause schizophrenic-like symptoms. Moreover, researchers also find abnormal electrical patterns, measured by an instrument called an EEG (electroencephalograph), in the limbic system of schizophrenic patients.

Abnormalities in the Cerebrum

Another common structural abnormality in the schizophrenic brain is in a structure known as the inferior parietal lobe (IPL) of the cerebral cortex. The cortex is the outer layer—the gray matter—of the cerebrum, and is responsible for conscious thought.

The IPL translates sensory information into a picture of the world at a given moment. A recent study at Johns Hopkins University found that the IPL in many schizophrenics is smaller than normal. The researchers believe this may account for some of the distortions of reality experienced by people who have schizophrenia.

The researchers in this study also discovered that the IPL in schizophrenic men is different from the IPL in normal people and in schizophrenic women. In normal people the IPL is larger on the left side of the brain. In schizophrenic men it is larger on the right side. In another study the same researchers found that Wernicke's area, a section of the cerebral cortex important in speech and language, is also built backwards in schizophrenic men. The scientists think these findings help explain why men with schizophrenia are more likely to be totally disabled by the disease and respond less readily to medication than women do. "Women's brains are apparently better protected from whatever schizophrenia does,"[13] says lead researcher Dr. Godfrey Pearlson.

Oddities in How the Brain Works

Besides structural differences, schizophrenia involves oddities in how the brain works. PET scans, for example, have shown that many people with schizophrenia have lower than normal blood flow and unusual nerve connections to areas in the thalamus, a brain stem region important in screening sensations, pleasure, and pain, in the cerebellum, responsible for balance and coordination, and in the prefrontal cortex. Doctors believe these differences explain some of the thought distortions, attention deficits, problem-solving difficulties, and motion problems seen in schizophrenia.

Other interesting PET and MRI studies are beginning to provide doctors with a look at the causes of hallucinations experienced by many schizophrenics. A recent MRI study in Great Britain by Dr. Robin Murray and his colleagues, for instance, discovered that the auditory cortex is active both when schizophrenics hear real voices and when they report having auditory hallucinations. In normal people this area is active only when the person hears real voices. "The schizophrenic brain reacts as if unable to distinguish between its own internally generated speech and actual, audible speech,"[14] the scientists suggest.

Experts eventually hope to establish links between many more of the symptoms and subtypes of schizophrenia and specific brain functions. One recent study, for example, indicates that negative symptoms are linked to unusually low activity in a brain structure called the prefrontal cortex. Such discoveries, researchers hope, will provide new understanding of the causes of schizophrenia and possibly lead to treatments for the disease.

Prenatal Damage

Doctors believe that many of the abnormal brain activities and structures in schizophrenics develop before or during birth. There is considerable evidence that a difficult childbirth may result in brain damage associated with the disease in individuals who are predisposed to schizophrenia because of heredity. Studies show that birth complications like a breech birth, use of forceps during delivery, prolonged labor, and lack of oxygen for the fetus are associated with a high incidence of schizophrenia later in life.

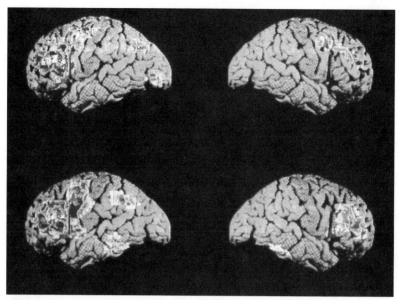

When performing certain tasks—speaking or listening, for example—the activity in a schizophrenic's brain (bottom) is different from that of a normal brain.

Researchers suspect that prior to birth, exposure to certain viruses or other conditions like poor nutrition may also cause these types of brain abnormalities. Yet, scientists believe, this brain damage does not usually produce schizophrenia before adolescence because special conditions are needed to activate the disease. This theory is supported by a 1998 Yale University study which used X rays to damage the brains of monkeys during fetal development. The monkeys seemed normal during childhood but started showing schizophrenic-like symptoms in adolescence. The researchers think that the triggering conditions during puberty may include hormones that become active at this time, myelination (the completion of the shield called the myelin sheath around nerve cells), and the loss of some nerve cell connections that begins during the teen years.

The Role of Prenatal Viruses

One of the primary prenatal influences being studied is viruses. Researchers suspect that several viruses may play a role in schizophrenia, though none are yet proven to be responsible. Laboratory tests reveal that schizophrenics have greater than normal antibodies to a wide range of viruses that could cause brain damage.

Some of the viruses suspected of being associated with schizophrenia are cold and flu viruses. Evidence implicating these pathogens comes from studies demonstrating that when such viruses strike a mother during the third to seventh month of pregnancy, the virus can infect the fetus and attack certain areas of the brain that are involved in schizophrenia.

In one long-term study done in Finland, researchers found that a large number of children of mothers exposed to a severe flu epidemic developed schizophrenia over the next twenty-six years. Related studies show similar increases in the incidence of schizophrenia among children born during times when there were epidemics of flu, measles, chicken pox, and polio viruses.

In another line of inquiry, Drs. E. Fuller Torrey and Robert Yolken have theorized that viruses that can be transmitted from cats to pregnant women may be important. They point out that cats were rarely kept as indoor pets in Europe or America until the nineteenth century, the same time when the incidence of schizophrenia suddenly increased dramatically.

Adding strength to the possible connection between cats and schizophrenia, the incidence of schizophrenia increased the most in places where pet cats became the most popular. This pattern continues to hold. Ireland and Sweden, where house cats are abundant, still have the highest rates of schizophrenia in the world. In the United States, New England and the Pacific Coast states have more pet cats, and more schizophrenia, than anywhere else in the country.

Still, Torrey and Yolken emphasize that "there is no reason at this time for anyone to change behavior towards cats or cat ownership"[15] until further research proves a connection between feline viruses and schizophrenia, but their ideas have added a new avenue of inquiry for researchers seeking to identify the viruses that may contribute to schizophrenia.

New Research

Exciting new research offers clues as to how prenatal viruses or other events in the uterus may affect the developing schizophrenic brain. According to the American Psychiatric Association, "The genes of people with schizophrenia may tell the immune system to attack the brain after a viral infection. This theory is supported by the discovery that the blood of people with schizophrenia contains antibodies—immune system cells—specific to the brain."[16]

Another line of research is looking at how prenatal events influence the development of nerve cells. One way might involve an alteration in the way fetal neurons find their correct places in various brain regions. Psychiatrist Godfrey Pearlson, M.D., a lead investigator in the Johns Hopkins study of the IPL in schizophrenics, says, "It's likely that something goes awry with the ways neurons migrate to the IPL and other brain regions, or how they form connections."[17]

Other research suggests that disorganized patterns and abnormal shapes and sizes in neurons at the fetal stage of development may be

Some researchers wonder if there is a link between cats and schizophrenia.

linked to the onset of schizophrenia later on. Scientists believe a chemical called reelin may be partly responsible for these abnormalities, since reelin plays a vital role in positioning nerve cells and in the growth of dendrites (branches that extend from nerve cells). Schizophrenics' brains have less than normal amounts of reelin, and researchers suspect that adverse prenatal events, such as exposure to a virus, may cause genetically susceptible people to reduce their reelin output.

Neurotransmitters and Schizophrenia

One particularly promising line of research regarding brain chemicals involved in schizophrenia is looking at how neurotransmitters, the chemicals that conduct electrical signals from one neuron to another, affect the disease. When certain neurotransmitters are deficient or overly abundant, neurons cannot communicate in a normal fashion, and severe disruptions in thinking and behavior can result. Doctors now believe that many of the symptoms found in schizophrenia are related to abnormal levels of neurotransmitters. Neurotransmitters are of particular interest to doctors who work with schizophrenics because the drugs being used to treat the disease act primarily on these substances.

Dr. Arvid Carlsson in Sweden first investigated the role of neurotransmitters in schizophrenia in 1957. Carlsson discovered the neurotransmitter dopamine and later proved that chlorpromazine, one of the first drugs that effectively treated schizophrenia, eliminated some symptoms by blocking dopamine receptors in the brain. Dopamine receptors are areas on neurons where dopamine from other neurons attaches. The human brain has five types of these receptors which scientists label D1–D5.

Later research confirmed that the brains of schizophrenics contain too much dopamine. When given drugs that increase the amount of dopamine, people with schizophrenia experience a worsening of their symptoms. In addition, PET scans show that schizophrenic patients' dopamine receptors absorb more dopamine than those of normal people.

For a while doctors believed overproduction only of dopamine was responsible for schizophrenia, but recent research indicates

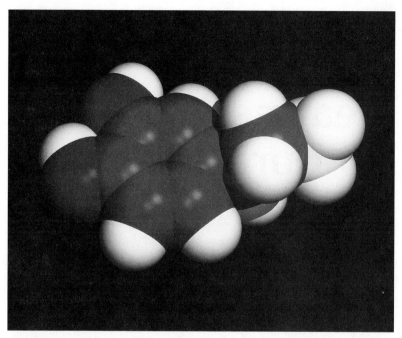

Doctors now believe that abnormal levels of neurotransmitters may play a role in schizophrenia.

other neurotransmitters are also involved. When drugs that increase the levels of the neurotransmitters glutamate and serotonin are ingested, symptoms of schizophrenia result, so researchers believe these brain chemicals play a role, too. Doctors hope that studies of these and other neurotransmitters will eventually lead to a better understanding of the causes and possible treatments of the disease.

Chapter 3

Treatment but No Cure

S CHIZOPHRENIA HAS NO known cure, so the goal of treatment is to get the patient out of the acute phase and into the stable phase of the disease so the individual can lead a productive life. This process involves the doctor, who is usually a psychiatrist, working with the patient to develop a long-term plan of action that includes regularly taking medication, keeping appointments with doctors and other therapists, and watching for danger signals, such as increasing anxiety, that may indicate a relapse.

Besides setting up and monitoring each patient's treatment plan, the psychiatrist is generally responsible for connecting the patient with other professionals who function as a team in working with the schizophrenic. This can occur either in a hospital or outpatient setting depending on the patient's needs. Many clinics have case managers who also help coordinate a patient's therapy.

Hospitalization

Experts say the most effective treatment plans combine medication with psychotherapy, education, and social rehabilitation programs that address the living skills and emotional needs of the patient. Regardless of the ultimate design of the individual treatment program, therapy usually begins in a psychiatric hospital.

Hospitalization is usually required for several reasons. First of all, the doctor must conduct medical tests to rule out other possible causes of the patient's behavior. Second, settling on the best medications and dosages involves considerable trial and error, and in the meantime the patient needs to be closely observed. Third, patients may be unable to attend to their own needs for nutrition and hygiene during the acute phase of their illness. Patients in the acute phase may also be so far removed from reality that they can injure themselves or others.

Mental hospitals and psychiatric wards in regular hospitals usually have a locked ward for agitated or confused patients. There are also additional restraints for patients who pose a danger to themselves or others. These restraints include leather ankle and wrist holders, and jackets called straitjackets that keep the arms next to the patient's sides. Hospital staff can also put dangerous patients in special padded rooms called seclusion rooms.

Patients must often remain hospitalized during the next phase of the disease, the stabilization phase, while they gradually regain the ability to care for themselves. Most doctors try to follow the American Psychiatric Association's guideline for providing treatment in the "least restrictive setting" possible during each phase of the disease.

In order to conduct medical tests and monitor medications, some hospitalization is usually required when treating schizophrenia.

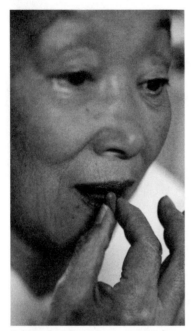

Schizophrenic patients must take their medications regularly.

Usually, therefore, when a doctor feels that a patient is stabilized enough to continue their therapy on an outpatient basis, the patient can be released from the hospital.

In the stabilization phase, according to the American Psychiatric Association, "the aims of treatment are to minimize stress on the patient and provide support to minimize the likelihood of relapse, enhance the patient's adaptation to life in the community, and facilitate continued reduction in symptoms and consolidation of remission [absence of symptoms]."[18]

The psychiatrist's goal is ultimately to help the patient reach the stable phase, in which the person can most often be treated as an outpatient. During this phase the objective is to help the schizophrenic maintain a good quality of life, which includes regularly taking medications and sticking with a prescribed psychotherapy and rehabilitation plan. Some patients achieve complete remission in the stable phase. Others experience negative symptoms that worsen during this phase; this can place the patient in the category of a residual schizophrenic. Still others go through cycles of remission and relapse, where the acute phase returns after varying lengths of time.

These individual differences in patterns of recovery are part of what makes schizophrenia such a complicated disease to treat. But as physicians learn more about how various types of patients respond to treatment, they are better able to predict who is likely to recover and remain in the stable phase.

Predicting Success

While it is difficult for doctors to predict how successful any treatment plan will be in an individual case, certain factors point to a positive or negative outcome. Treatment is most likely to be successful when the schizophrenic understands and takes an active role in the process. When the doctor's team makes an effort to answer the person's questions and explain the reason for using certain drugs and other therapies, the patient is more motivated to stick with the program and try to get better.

People who were well-adjusted before the illness struck also tend to get better with treatment. For example, individuals who did well in school and made friends easily are more likely to respond favorably to treatment than those who have a history of being withdrawn and in trouble.

Other variables that seem to determine how well treatment works are the patient's gender, marital status, age, how quickly the disease progressed, recent stressful events, general physical health, and the type of schizophrenia the patient has. For reasons that are imperfectly understood, women respond better to treatment than men; married patients, probably because they receive some emotional support from a spouse, respond better than single patients. People who experience

Certain factors like a patient's marital status seem to play a role in treating the disease.

a sudden onset of symptoms rather than having the disease progress gradually also tend to benefit more from treatment, as do those whose symptoms seemed to be triggered by some stressful event. Perhaps not surprisingly, being in good physical health helps. And, having the paranoid subtype also increases a patient's chances of successful treatment.

Treatment is less likely to be successful for people who have a family history of schizophrenia, those diagnosed with disorganized subtype, anyone who shows brain abnormalities on a CT scan, patients who take a long time to respond to medication, and those who are unaware that something is wrong with them. Doctors also find that the earlier someone develops schizophrenia, the less chance there is of medications or other treatments being effective. The most difficult cases to treat are those that began when the patient was younger than fifteen. Although researchers have no proof as to why this is so, they suspect that cases that develop earlier involve more profound brain damage.

Early Attempts at Treatment

Regardless of the variables at work, before the discovery of modern drugs and treatment plans in the last half of the twentieth century, very few schizophrenics got better. Faced with what seemed an incurable and untreatable illness, many doctors tried treatments that today seem dangerous and even abusive.

Some of the earliest attempts at treatment, such as injecting bacteria or poisons like turpentine to create a fever, were tried because they seemed to work for other mental illness. Although this treatment worked for a disorder called neurosyphilitis, it did nothing to help schizophrenics.

Faced with the failure of such rudimentary medical treatments, during the late nineteenth and early twentieth centuries some doctors began to experiment with operating on the brain to cure schizophrenia. In 1936 the American neurologists Walter Freeman and James Watts coined the term "lobotomy" to describe a new surgery that involved cutting out a portion of the brain's frontal lobes. The physicians reasoned that, since the procedure calmed aggressive animals, it would also calm agitated schizophrenics. Lobotomies did quiet many aggressive or frantic schizophrenics, but it also destroyed their thinking and social skills. Despite these drawbacks, doctors continued to perform many lobotomies until more effective treatments were discovered in the 1950s.

Convulsion Therapy

Another treatment that became popular in the 1930s was convulsion therapy, which involved injecting camphor, which caused seizures. The rationale behind this treatment was the observation that patients with epilepsy had fewer seizures if they developed schizophrenia. Psychiatrists hoped that causing seizures in schizophrenics who did not have epilepsy might somehow help these patients recover from their mental illness.

Some doctors found that these injections did indeed eliminate schizophrenic symptoms in many patients. But the camphor produced unpleasant side effects like vomiting and pain in the muscles where it was injected. It was also not a reliable way of inducing seizures, so they tried another chemical called Metrazol. This also was unreliable and had horrible side effects, as patients turned blue from lack of oxygen and were in agony during the convulsions. Nevertheless, quite a few doctors throughout the world began using this therapy.

ECT

Patients loathed and dreaded Metrazol injections so much that they had to be tied down and forced to endure the procedure. In response, psychiatrists began looking for a less unpleasant way of causing convulsions, and in the late 1930s, Dr. Ugo Cerletti of Rome developed a method of giving patients electric shocks to produce the seizures. In 1938, Cerletti and his assistants found that attaching electrodes to a patient's temples and delivering a strong electric shock to the brain caused a seizure and immediate unconsciousness. The procedure came to be known as electroconvulsive therapy (ECT). After giving one schizophrenic man eleven ECT treatments, Cerletti claimed the patient was free of any schizophrenic symptoms and able to leave the hospital. Some of the symptoms later returned, but the man did not have to be rehospitalized.

No one knew how and why ECT helped this patient, but doctors who heard of the outcome began using ECT on other schizophrenics. The fact that ECT caused immediate unconsciousness made it less unpleasant than Metrazol injections, so patients were more willing to undergo the therapy.

ECT did seem to help in many cases, but the side effects of memory loss and injury while thrashing around during the convulsion made it a dangerous procedure nonetheless. In the 1940s doctors began using sedatives and muscle-paralyzing drugs to lessen these injuries, but the memory loss remained a serious risk.

In the 1970s, public concern about the overuse of ECT led the federal government and states to pass laws restricting its use, and today it is rarely used. Many modern doctors still claim the benefits outweigh the risks, however, so sometimes they perform ECT on schizophrenics who are not helped by medication.

Today, ECT is rarely used as a treatment for schizophrenia.

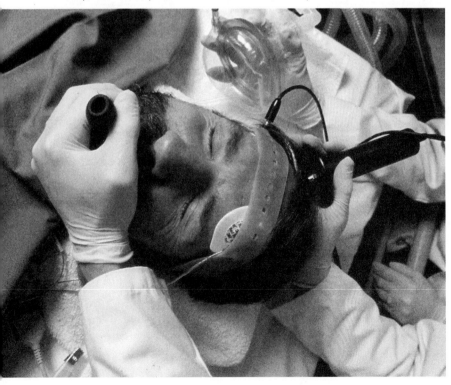

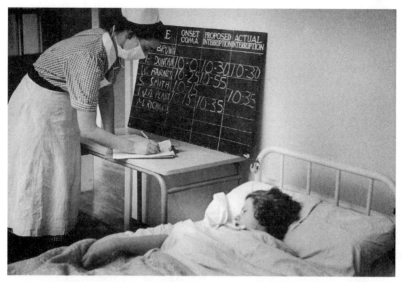

Early treatments for schizophrenia included insulin coma therapy (pictured) and high dosages of sleeping pills.

Early Drug Treatments

Even as they were trying to treat schizophrenia by inducing seizures, doctors also were trying a variety of drugs, beginning in the 1900s. Among the drugs used were large doses of sleeping pills that put the schizophrenic into a deep sleep for several days. The rationale for using these sedatives was to try to calm patients enough so they would benefit from talking to a psychotherapist. The procedure seemed to reduce symptoms in many patients, but unfortunately about 5 percent of the people given the "prolonged sleep" treatment died, so researchers continued to look for safer, more effective drugs.

In the 1930s psychiatrists began using a technique called insulin coma therapy. Insulin, a hormone necessary for keeping blood sugar levels normal, was already widely used to treat diabetes, and doctors were aware that too much insulin could send a patient into a coma.

The Austrian psychiatrist Manfred Sakel decided to try using insulin to induce comas in his schizophrenic patients and found that 70 percent of them awoke symptom-free after about twenty treatments. Another 18 percent experienced what Sakel called a "social remission," which enabled them to function better around other people.

Other doctors were amazed at these results, and by 1939 most mental hospitals throughout the world had opened insulin coma clinics. Despite the successful treatment rate, about 1 percent of the patients died during the procedure, so insulin coma therapy was discontinued after safer drug treatments became available in the 1950s.

The Pharmacologic Revolution

In 1951 the French surgeon Henri Laborit was experimenting with antihistamines (drugs that control allergic reactions) to help calm his patients before surgery. He found that a new antihistamine called chlorpromazine made people both calm and "disinterested." Laborit suggested that the drug might be useful in treating schizophrenia, and psychiatrists Jean Delay and Pierre Deniker began testing it at the Saint Anne Mental Hospital in 1952.

One of Delay and Deniker's patients was a fifty-seven-year-old schizophrenic named Giovanni. This man was severely delusional and showed odd and irrational behaviors like walking around with a flowerpot on his head while talking nonsense. The doctors gave Giovanni chlorpromazine and nine days later his symptoms disappeared entirely. He was sent home from the hospital three weeks later, and his remission lasted as long as he kept taking the drug on a regular basis.

Other doctors began to administer the drug to their patients and had similarly quick and dramatic results. Never before had any drug made the symptoms of schizophrenia go away so safely and rapidly, and soon chlorpromazine led to a whole new class of safe, effective treatments for the disease. "Chlorpromazine initiated a revolution in psychiatry, comparable to the introduction of penicillin in general medicine,"[19] says psychiatrist Dr. Edward Shorter in his book *A History of Psychiatry*.

The Nature of Neuroleptics

After the discovery of chlorpromazine, scientists developed several similar drugs for treating schizophrenia. These drugs, called neuroleptics or antipsychotics, continue to be used for treating the disease today. Overall, 60 to 70 percent of patients who take these drugs achieve a complete remission or have only mild symptoms after six weeks of treatment. Most of the remaining patients still show moderate to severe psychotic symptoms, and about 5 percent actually get worse from these medications. Still, antipsychotics are the most effective treatment available for schizophrenia.

Antipsychotics work on all subtypes of schizophrenia, with of course different medicines working best for different people. Doctors believe a patient's unique body chemistry determines which drug works best and most quickly. Some patients start to get better within hours; for others it takes weeks or months to show improvement. Doctors may have to try several different drugs before finding one that helps a particular patient. As a result, simply arriving at the proper dosage of the proper drug can take months.

Physicians do not fully understand how antipsychotics work, but they do know that at least part of their action is related to blocking the brain's dopamine receptors. For example, a recent study in which patients taking the antipsychotic drug haloperidol were examined through PET scans found that the more haloperidol stuck to D2 receptors in the brain, the more a patient's condition improved.

When treating patients, doctors may have to try several different drugs before finding one that helps.

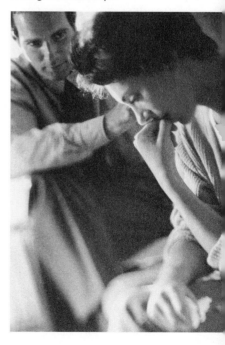

But other studies indicate dopamine blocking is not the whole story. Researchers know that even some drugs that completely block dopamine receptors within twenty-four hours do not give people relief from symptoms for several weeks. Moreover, an antipsychotic medication called clozapine, a very weak dopamine blocker, is very effective in treating schizophrenia.

Doctors now believe that antipsychotics also work on other neurotransmitters besides dopamine, and current research is attempting to find out exactly which neurotransmitters are involved. Some researchers also theorize that antipsychotics destroy certain viruses that may be linked to schizophrenia, but this is unproven.

Conventional Antipsychotics

There are two main categories of antipsychotic drugs: conventional and atypical. Examples of conventional antipsychotics are haloperidol and chlorpromazine. These drugs are effective in reducing positive symptoms, though they do not work well on negative symptoms. Thus, they are more likely to reduce delusions and hallucinations but not blunted emotions or behaviors such as prolonged silence.

Although they are clearly effective, one problem is that these drugs are given daily in liquid or tablet form. Many schizophrenics, however, are afraid to take medicine because their paranoid delusions lead them to believe the doctor is trying to poison them with the medications. Other patients are so impaired by disorganized thoughts that they are incapable of taking the medication on a regular basis. For such people who cannot or will not take their prescribed oral antipsychotics, doctors can administer injections that last one to four weeks. These injections, called depot formulations, allow the body to store the medicine, which works as the patient's body gradually metabolizes it. The problem remains, however, of seeing to it that the patient gets the injections on a regular basis.

Another major problem with conventional antipsychotics is the discomfort of frequent side effects. These include restlessness, dry mouth, impotence, blurred vision, constipation, and weight gain. One common side effect causes muscles to "freeze," resulting in extreme rigidity of the body, tremors, abnormally slow movement, and involuntary muscle twitches. Other patients experience involuntary movements of the mouth, tongue, and lips, like grimacing, lip smacking, and tongue rolling. Psychiatrists note that many schizophrenics experience these symptoms even without antipsychotic medications; however, the drugs can make these symptoms worse.

Many of these side effects can be reduced by changing a patient's medication or dosage, but often they remain unpleasant enough to make many patients stop taking the drugs. As one woman states about her antipsychotic medicine, "It relieves my mental stress, but I hate my bodily responses to it and the dulling of my healthy emotions. Therefore I stop using the drug as soon as the storms in my mind subside."[20]

Unfortunately for patients who do this, discontinuing these medicines can have disastrous effects. Studies show that 60 to 80 percent of patients who stop taking the prescibed antipsychotics experience a relapse of the disease within a year. This is why motivating schizophrenics to faithfully take their medicine is a priority for doctors, caregivers, and families.

Atypical Antipsychotics

A newer class of drugs called atypical antipsychotics tends to have fewer side effects than conventional ones, so they are often prescribed when this is a problem. Atypical antipsychotics include clozapine, risperidone, and olanzapine. They are called "atypical" because, unlike conventional antipsychotics, they do not work primarily by blocking dopamine receptors. Instead, atypical drugs seem to block receptors for serotonin, acetylcholine, and histamine, but exactly how they work is unknown.

These atypical drugs work as well as conventional ones on positive symptoms and are more effective in treating negative symptoms. A recent study showed that clozapine and olanzapine also reduced the suicide risk in many schizophrenics; this indicates that they affect mood and outlook as well as treat the usual symptoms of schizophrenia.

While atypical antipsychotics rarely cause the annoying side effects involving rigidness and repetitive mouth movements, they can produce other side effects such as drowsiness, nausea, weight gain, dizziness, fast heart rate, breathing problems, and decreased blood pressure. Clozapine is also known to occasionally cause seizures, blood clots, and a fatal blood disorder that involves a decrease in the number of white blood cells. Patients who take this drug must have weekly blood tests to make sure they are not getting this dangerous condition. Because of the risk, some doctors will not prescribe clozapine except in cases where other antipsychotic drugs fail to work.

Long-Term Treatment with Drugs

Long-term treatment with such potent and potentially dangerous drugs means that schizophrenics must be closely monitored by a health professional. Patients must undergo frequent blood tests to ensure that toxic concentrations of the drugs are not building up in the bloodstream. The physician also must assess how well the medication is controlling the patient's schizophrenic symptoms and make changes in the dosage if necessary. Depending on the individual patient, daily, weekly, or monthly follow-up appointments may be necessary.

In addition to antipsychotic drugs, the physician may also prescribe other medicines as needed. If the patient is depressed or anxious, the doctor can order antidepressants or antianxiety drugs. If the person has severe side effects from the antipsychotics, drugs that block the neurotransmitter acetylcholine can often help. Lithium, a medication commonly used to treat a mental illness called manic depressive psychosis, is sometimes given to schizophrenics in combination with other antipsychotic medicines.

Treatment Beyond Drugs

Drugs are only part of a total treatment plan for schizophrenia, however. Once the symptoms of the disease are being controlled with appropriate medications, other forms of therapy aimed at helping the patient deal with the social and emotional aspects of schizophrenia may be prescribed.

For many years psychiatrists and psychoanalysts used traditional Freudian psychoanalysis in hopes of uncovering and treating the underlying cause of the patient's symptoms. Studies have proved that such psychoanalysis is ineffective in helping schizophrenics, but other forms of psychotherapy where a patient talks with a doctor have been found to be very valuable when combined with a drug treatment plan. Examples of effective psychotherapies are cognitive therapy, which focuses on getting patients to reorganize their ways of thinking about their lives, and group therapy, where patients meet with therapists and other patients. Different therapies or combinations of therapies work best for different individuals.

In cognitive therapy, a therapist might attempt to help schizophrenics consistently think of their medication regimen as a positive step toward recovery rather than as a distasteful burden. Another typical focus may be on changing schizophrenic ways of thinking

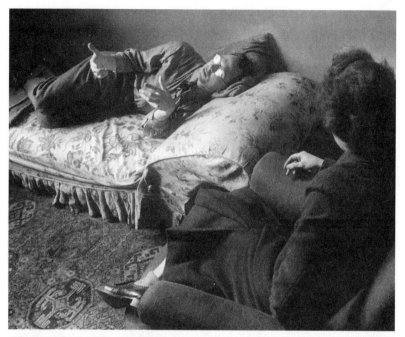

When combined with a drug treatment plan, psychotherapy can be valuable to schizophrenic patients.

about themselves so they will feel confident enough to try to get a job or venture into social relationships.

In group therapy, patients themselves often help therapists conduct sessions so people with similar problems can offer constructive advice and compassion. Some group therapy programs involve patients forming clubs and special interest groups to introduce worthwhile pastimes into their lives. Others include activities like role-playing to help the patients gain social skills.

Experts emphasize that enabling schizophrenics to talk about their concerns and symptoms will not make these symptoms go away, but in many cases this can help the schizophrenic become less fearful and continue to function despite their presence. Sometimes having someone there to listen simply provides needed emotional support. Responding to a book she read that stated psychotherapy is useless for schizophrenics, one patient asked of the author, "How can he even suggest that without knowing me, the one over here in this corner, who finds a lot of support, understanding, and acceptance with my therapist?"[21] Many other patients share this view that psychotherapy is an important component in their individual treatment plan.

Modifying Behavior

In addition to helping a schizophrenic understand and deal with the social and emotional problems that go along with the disease, psychotherapy can help the person change behaviors that are unacceptable or damaging to the individual's ability to cope. Psychologists have developed a variety of behavior modification techniques for this purpose. Most involve the concept of reinforcing acceptable behaviors with appropriate rewards.

Psychologist Dr. Susan Baur, author of *The Dinosaur Man*, set up a behavior modification program in a mental hospital to help schizophrenics learn skills for independent living. In her words:

Functioning independently is the goal of therapy for schizophrenics.

The goal was to introduce a pervasive system of rewards and punishments that would encourage chronic patients to say please and thank you, wear socks, take their antipsychotic medications, keep their flies zipped up, and in a dozen other ways conform to our visible standards of sanity. Thus rehabilitated, the reasoning went, they would move into foster homes and would have a better chance of fitting into the community.[22]

But as Baur found out and many other therapists would soon discover, oftentimes patients do not care about learning social graces and acting sane. Some just want someone to listen to stories about their fantasy worlds, while others are not stable enough to understand what therapy is all about. Others simply do not care about fitting into the world around them. Baur observed:

Among chronically ill patients who had lived for ten or twenty years on the back wards, for example, few seemed to want to learn what I was supposed to teach them, and even those willing to modify their behavior in order to leave the hospital were not captivated by learning how to ask directions to the bus station or how to start a conversation. Those weren't their goals.[23]

But as experts point out, even in these types of cases where the therapist's goals are different from those of the patient, many schizophrenics benefit from having a professional listen to them, offer appropriate encouragement, and discuss how and why certain behaviors can be changed if the person does recover to the point that he or she wishes to function outside a hospital.

Rehabilitation Therapy

Ultimately, of course, it is the ability to function in society that is the goal of therapy. With this in mind, many hospitals and outpatient clinics offer schizophrenic patients social and vocational rehabilitation programs. These programs are usually administered by social workers and rehabilitation specialists who aim to help patients learn the skills they need to interact with others, get a job, and live independently. Some of these programs are geared toward individuals; others are run in group settings.

Some of the skills taught include personal care, money management, shopping skills, and various job skills. Therapists use behavioral learning techniques like coaching, modeling correct behaviors, and positive reinforcement to teach these skills. Studies show that schizophrenics who stick with these programs are more likely to get and keep a job, learn to live independently, and avoid relapses of the disease.

Some of these rehabilitation plans include the patient's family as well. One approach, called psychoeducational family therapy, teaches family members communication, coping, and problem-solving skills in an effort to involve the family in the schizophrenic's rehabilitation. This therapy can be highly effective: One study found that patients who participated in both psychoeducational family therapy and social skills training had zero relapses over one year.

Comprehensive Therapy Packages

Numerous studies have indicated that comprehensive therapy programs that include treating the social, psychological, and medical aspects of schizophrenia offer patients the best chances of leading productive lives. Oftentimes, though, the costs of such services prevent many schizophrenics from participating. Since medical insurance plans frequently do not cover all, if any, mental health services, families must absorb expenses, which experts have estimated can be as high as fifty thousand dollars per year. In fact, many families, in attempting to pay for a schizophrenic's ongoing treatment, face complete financial ruin. In some cases, parents of schizophrenic children or teenagers have to resort to extreme measures like giving up custody so the government will pay for treatment.

Often, patients are caught in a bind from which there seems to be no escape. Schizophrenic adults who are unable to work cannot obtain health insurance through an employer, but in order to qualify for government medical funding they must be practically destitute. As a result, people who have limited savings but no insurance often must go without treatment. Those who do obtain government assistance find that sometimes it is discontinued when laws concerning Social Security Disability Insurance and welfare programs are changed. Battling the bureaucracy in an attempt to procure adequate treat-

Studies show that comprehensive therapy programs offer patients the best chance of leading productive lives.

ment can easily overwhelm mentally ill individuals and their families to the point that they give up and stop trying to get help.

Mental health advocacy groups are working diligently to change laws and medical insurance coverage policies so all schizophrenics have access to comprehensive treatment packages. Some states have recently enacted legislation requiring private medical insurers to pay for mental health care just as they would cover physical illnesses. Still, the time when everyone with schizophrenia has an opportunity to benefit from treatment for their disease lies in the future.

Chapter 4

Living with Schizophrenia

S INCE SCHIZOPHRENIA HAS no known cure, people with the disease face many ongoing challenges in their daily lives, even when treatment is effective. Besides the constant personal struggles inherent in coping with a frightening array of symptoms, many schizophrenics must depend on family members or social services for basic necessities like food and shelter. Added to these difficulties are the isolation and rejection that often make living with schizophrenia an unending battle for survival in a world that seems hostile and foreign.

One significant obstacle for many schizophrenics resulted from laws initiated in responce to the antipsychiatry movement in the 1960s. These laws mandated that as many patients as possible be released from mental hospitals. What the laws often failed to take into account was the patients' ability to function outside of these facilities. Once on their own, many schizophrenics did not take the medicines they needed to control their symptoms, and often they became homeless or committed crimes as a result. The hoped-for community outpatient programs that would take over and treat these people did not materialize, and doctors finally started readmitting many schizophrenics to mental hospitals in the late 1980s.

Even so, a large number of schizophrenics are still homeless. About 100,000 currently live on the street or in homeless shelters in the United States. Unsupervised, they often get into trouble. Another 100,000 live in jails and prisons. Most have been incarcerated for minor offenses like trespassing or public intoxication, but some are extremely dangerous and have committed violent crimes.

Other living situations include about 150,000 schizophrenics in nursing homes, 300,000 in group homes or other supervised living facilities, 50,000 living independently, 100,000 in mental hospitals, and 500,000 living with family members.

Supervised Living

Some schizophrenics are stable enough to live outside a hospital, but still require varying levels of care. This can range from full-time care in a nursing home to care as needed in a group home, foster home, halfway house, or board and care home. The services and quality of care offered in these settings vary widely, but in general, residents of these supervised accommodations receive a room, meals, help with taking medicines, and assistance with daily chores as needed.

About 100,000 schizophrenics are homeless in the United States.

The care provided by such facilities is itself of considerable concern in society today. Experts report that some of these residences give excellent care while others neglect or even abuse patients, who are often unaware of how to report such abuses. Mental health advocacy groups are attempting to correct these problems by seeking vigorous enforcement of laws that regulate these types of facilities.

Another issue that often confronts the mentally ill is the availability of treatment facilities. Supervised care homes often must overcome the fear and mistrust of the mentally ill on the part of local residents. Mental health experts find that many communities are reluctant to license halfway houses or board and care homes because they worry that property values will suffer or that the public will be victimized by patients prone to violence. However, scientific research has shown that property values generally do not decline. Moreover, the American Psychiatric Association asserts that "As long as people maintain their medication, studies have shown that those with serious mental illnesses are no more dangerous than the general population."[24] Advocacy groups such as the National Alliance for the Mentally Ill are, accordingly, working to educate local planners and decision makers in the hope that they will be more likely to allow these much-needed facilities in their communities.

Schizophrenics Who Live Independently

Not every schizophrenic requires the kind of care offered in supervised living situations and can live independently. Schizophrenics who live independently should ideally be able to care for their own needs like grooming, shopping, cooking, cleaning, and taking their medication. Some do fine caring for themselves for long periods of time but must occasionally be rehospitalized when they experience relapses—acute psychotic episodes. Still others remain in remission and can lead fairly normal lives as long as they regularly see a doctor for follow-up care.

Some independent schizophrenics are able to work and support themselves, while others rely on federal or state government benefits like Social Security Disability Insurance, Supplemental Security Income, Medicaid, or housing assistance programs. Several researchers have reported that patients who work tend to feel better about themselves, are more likely to carefully follow their doctors' orders, and

Holding a regular job gives schizophrenics a sense of accomplishment and independence.

generally enjoy a better quality of life than those who are unemployed. One 1998 study in Great Britain found that among schizophrenics interviewed in the United States, Great Britain, and Switzerland,

> employed patients displayed less psychopathology [psychotic symptoms] and significant advantages in terms of objective and subjective measures of income and well-being. They were also more likely to stress the importance of work. These results suggest that work is associated with a markedly better quality of life for people with schizophrenia.[25]

The responsibility of holding a regular job keeps schizophrenics busy, gives them a sense of accomplishment, and motivates them not to let a chronic disease defeat them. These qualities may in fact be part of what allows patients to hold a job in the first place, but either way, being employed is a positive force in the schizophrenic's daily life. This is why many doctors and others involved in schizophrenia care encourage and help patients to learn marketable skills and get jobs.

Keeping busy with other worthwhile pastimes like going to school, doing volunteer work, and attending support group meetings also helps many independent schizophrenics cope with their illness, diminishing some of the feelings of isolation many endure. Groups like Schizophrenics Anonymous (SA), an international support group run by schizophrenics, give many people the strength and know-how to live successfully and even help fellow patients recover from the disease. Jamie, a member of SA who counsels other schizophrenics, says of the group he attends, "It has given me a purpose in life and made me realize that I have a lot to offer people. I don't worry anymore about feeling paranoid or get upset over everyday stressors, because there is so much to do, and I have people around me who understand what I experience." [26]

Recently, organizations besides patient support groups have become involved in trying to reduce the social isolation that frequently accompanies serious mental disorders. One example is the Friend-

Support groups help many schizophrenics feel better about themselves and cope with their disease.

ship Network in New York, which provides dating services for mentally ill people. This organization says it offers its members "a chance to develop or redevelop the social skills they may have forgotten and, eventually, to develop the self-confidence necessary to expand their social life beyond the Friendship Network. The Friendship Network offers members the option to have pen or phone pals as well."[27] In another type of program, sponsored by numerous social service and humane society groups, volunteers bring dogs to visit schizophrenics in the hope that these loving animals will help patients feel less isolated.

Living in a Mental Hospital

At the opposite end of the spectrum are patients whose symptoms are so severe that they need the care provided by public or private mental hospitals. Although for many schizophrenics, hospital care is a temporary accommodation just until symptoms are controlled, for others, treatment is ineffective and the schizophrenic may remain in the hospital for many years or even decades. Doctors and other caretakers continue to try to help these long-term hospital patients get better, but for some there is little that can be done and the hospital becomes a permanent home.

The basic therapeutic setup in most mental hospitals includes a primary nurse who coordinates each patient's care with a team of doctors, nurses, psychologists, and other therapists who teach living skills, job skills, group therapy, and lead activity groups. The primary nurse is often the one who gets to know the patient best and who is responsible for bringing any changes in behavior or problems with medication to the attention of the psychiatrist in charge of managing the person's medical needs.

Patients in a mental hospital are usually not confined to bed unless they are violent and must be forcibly restrained and medicated. Most stay in a ward where other patients eat and sleep, and each day they are encouraged to attend various therapy sessions and activities in other parts of the hospital. Patients are also not required to wear hospital gowns as is customary in most inpatient facilities, and oftentimes their attire reflects the disorganized nature of the illness. In her book *The Dinosaur Man*, therapist Dr. Susan Baur describes some

Schizophrenic patients whose symptoms are severe may live in public or private mental hospitals.

typical schizophrenics in the mental hospital where she worked: "Men commonly wore two or three shirts apiece, and women roped themselves into dresses that earlier had served as circus tents."[28]

Staff members and visitors to mental hospitals report that, as a result of the nature of severe psychiatric illnesses like schizophrenia, many patients display odd and socially unacceptable behaviors in addition to dressing in bizarre clothing. It is common to see patients talking to themselves, lying in the hallways, and smoking constantly. Some ignore other people; others badger those around them verbally or physically. Some eat all the time; others rarely eat anything. Many refuse to practice basic hygiene and grooming.

While these odd and often antisocial behaviors may be upsetting for mentally healthy people to see, the staffs of modern mental hospitals try not to forcibly interfere except for patients considered dangerous to themselves or others. Partly, at least, as a result of laws enacted in the mid-1900s to correct frequent abuses and the unnecessary restraint of harmless individuals in such facilities, caretakers today are very much aware of the requirement that they respect each patient's personal right to behave as they wish as long as no one is injured and no laws are broken.

Difficulties in Placing Schizophrenics in Mental Hospitals

Ironically, the laws designed to protect individual patients' rights can prevent schizophrenics from even getting hospital care. Most states have strict laws that prohibit mentally ill persons from being hospitalized against their will unless the individual is "gravely disabled" or is an immediate danger to themself or others, as determined by a judge or mental health commission. "Gravely disabled" refers to people who are totally incapable of making decisions and who cannot care for themselves. This presents a dilemma because many schizophrenics are unable to recognize the fact that they are sick and therefore cannot make a rational decision about beginning treatment for the disease.

For families and doctors trying to do something positive for a schizophrenic who desperately needs but refuses to accept treatment, the paradox these laws present is frustrating. As psychiatrist Dr. E. Fuller Torrey, a noted authority on schizophrenia, states, "Civil rights lawyers and 'patient advocates' regularly defend individuals' rights to be psychotic . . . for example in Wisconsin a public defender argued that an individual with schizophrenia who was mute and eating his feces was not a danger to himself; the judge accepted the defense and released the man."[29]

Those who believe that current laws poorly serve both the mentally ill and the public point to occasional cases in which people should have been hospitalized but were not, leading to tragedy. One such case involved a Utah man named Ronnie Lee Kilgrow. Kilgrow strangled his ex-wife and choked their son into unconsciousness to save them from what he called a sky bomb. According to the Treatment Advocacy Center, a national group that seeks to improve existing laws related to treatment of the mentally ill:

Immediately prior to the slaying, Kilgrow had asked a highway patrol officer for his gun, telling the officer that he was afraid people were following him. The officer took Kilgrow to a mental health agency for evaluation, where he was seen by a social worker and released. John and Esther Wilson, the parents of Jayleen Kilgrow, Kilgrow's ex-wife, sued the mental health agency that had treated Kilgrow. They asserted that the agency had a professional duty—which it did not meet—to assess Kilgrow for violence and to require him to take his medication, given that he arrived as a consequence of having asked for a gun. A Utah judge dismissed their suit, accepting the argument of the defense attorney that, under state law, mental health professionals do not have a duty to warn anyone of a patient's potential for violence unless the patient constitutes a clear threat to a specific, identifiable victim.[30]

Sometimes families are forced to take drastic action in order to protect themselves and ensure that a schizophrenic relative receives necessary treatment. One California couple, frustrated in their attempts to force their violent schizophrenic son into a mental hospital, eventually

Unless patients are "gravely disabled," strict laws prohibit the mentally ill from being hospitalized against their will.

pressed felony charges against him, since under California law, a mentally ill felon must get psychiatric help. Lacking any alternatives for forcing their son into treatment, pressing felony charges became the only way of making sure this would happen.

Schizophrenics in the Family

Faced with the difficulty of hospitalizing a schizophrenic, many families must struggle with their own emotional trauma as they try to provide care for their loved one as best they can. Coming to grips with the reality of a severe mental illness often involves a grieving process similar to that which occurs when losing a family member. "In my personal experience, I went through a grieving process because our lives and our goals were suddenly changed. Many times this grieving process drastically changes a family's dynamics,"[31] explains Janice Holmes, a family advocate with the treatment and advocacy center known as Transitions Mental Health.

Mental health experts stress, however, that a family's ability to work through these emotional disturbances is critical for helping a schizophrenic live a productive life. While many people in this situation are so bewildered that they either deny that their loved one is ill or attempt to hide the patient at home, studies show that accepting that one's relative has the disease, learning about it, and taking steps to get medical help are key in promoting the schizophrenic's recovery. Recent research finds that schizophrenics whose families are ashamed of them feel more isolated, have a negative attitude about recovery, and are more likely to abuse drugs, whereas those with families who accept their illness are much more likely to achieve stability and control the disease.

Psychiatrist E. Fuller Torrey observes in his book *Surviving Schizophrenia*:

> Whenever I encounter such families [who deny or are ashamed about schizophrenia] I wish I could send them to a Buddhist monastery for a month. There they might learn the Oriental acceptance of life as it is, an invaluable attitude in surviving this disease. Such acceptance puts schizophrenia into perspective as one of life's great tragedies but stops it from becoming a festering sore eating away at life's very core.[32]

Day-to-Day Challenges for Families

Even families who accept the reality of living with schizophrenia and who try their hardest to help their mentally ill relative do not have an easy time. Often they are faced with doing the schizophrenic's cooking, cleaning, and shopping. Since many schizophrenics cannot drive, family members must transport the patient. They must also insure that the schizophrenic takes prescribed medicine and learn to be alert for any worsening symptoms or relapse.

Experts note that family members must also learn how to interact with the schizophrenic in a kind, caring, yet firm manner. Offering a highly structured environment where certain rules must be obeyed seems to work best. For instance, a family might develop a rule that the schizophrenic must not disrobe in front of visitors or face certain consequences.

Understanding the mental malfunctions involved in the disease can also help make the lives of the family and the mentally ill person easier. Normal peoples' brains screen and sort out incoming information, but schizophrenics' brains cannot do this. As a result, many schizophrenics cannot follow a conversation or even watch television because they are unable to mentally put the pieces together. This results in many unrelated thoughts and sensations going on at the same time. "My trouble is that I've got too many thoughts,"[33] says one schizophrenic man. Once family members understand this ongoing limitation in sorting and processing information, they can try to speak briefly and simply so the patient can understand them.

Another frequent problem encountered by schizophrenics is an intense blunting or heightening of their sensations. Many describe noises that seem louder than they used to be, colors that are brighter, or a slight touch to the skin as painful. Others' sensations are blunted so a shout may sound like a whisper or a normally painful experience like breaking a bone will not be felt at all. Caretakers who are aware of these malfunctions can try to avoid doing things that might cause the schizophrenic discomfort and can also watch for injuries that may have been sustained but which the patient may not feel.

Hand in hand with these perceptual abnormalities goes a distorted sense of self and a lack of understanding emotions that many schizophrenics report. The distorted sense of self makes the person unable to judge where their own body ends and other people or things begin. "I looked at my hands and I realized that they weren't part of my body, they were someone else's or they were a type of machinery like a robot,"[34] says schizophrenic patient Allison. Other common experiences include confusion about the right and left sides of the body and feeling like the face or body are deformed or stretched out. One woman was so confused about her own body that she believed she would not feel hungry anymore if her mother ate a meal.

The inability to understand emotions that often accompanies the disease results in inappropriate behaviors like laughing at a funeral or interpreting a smile as a threatening gesture. In studies where schizophrenics were asked to rate peoples' emotions from their facial expressions, most did not succeed. Normal people have little difficulty with this task.

Many schizophrenics report a distorted sense of self and an inability to understand emotions.

Experts point out that family members who understand that the jumble inside the schizophrenic's brain is likely to produce such distortions of emotions and sense of self are better prepared to handle such events in productive manner. Rather than ridiculing or arguing with the schizophrenic about these perceptions, mental health authorities recommend that the relative calmly state their own perceptions.

The same strategy is advised for dealing with the schizophrenic's delusions. "Instead of 'going along with' the person's delusions, family members or friends can tell the person they do not see things the same way or do not agree with his or her conclusions, while acknowledging that things may appear otherwise to the patient,"[35] says the National Institute of Mental Health. So if a schizophrenic refuses to enter a room because of a belief that it is infested with rats, a family member might ideally reply by saying that there are no rats visible.

Support Groups

Many families find mental health support groups extremely helpful in sharing information on coping strategies. A recent study by Dr. Phyllis Solomon of the University of Pennsylvania found that one major benefit of belonging to a support group was that family members felt like they were not alone in their struggles to interact with a mentally ill relative. Feeling isolated is reported to be a common reaction in such situations. As one woman revealed about her feelings after learning that a family member was seriously psychotic, "I found it difficult to talk to people who hadn't walked in my shoes." After joining a support group, though, she found, "For the first time, I could speak freely with other people who were facing the same problems."[36]

Some support groups are local chapters of national organizations like the National Alliance for the Mentally Ill (NAMI). Others are run by a local hospital or by state or county mental health departments. Some are informal groups run by health professionals or by the members themselves. Some support groups are designed for entire families, while others are solely for spouses, parents, or siblings of schizophrenics.

Support groups can help the family members of a schizophrenic.

General Issues of Living with Schizophrenia

Support groups can also help family members understand and facilitate a treatment regimen. It is helpful for the family to understand, for example, that establishing a regular daily routine is one useful practice that can help the patient cope with some of the unsettling confusion that accompanies the disease. Schizophrenics who are able to predict what they will be doing and when tend to function in a more stable manner.

A strategy for dealing with stress is also a stabilizing influence for a schizophrenic and can help the person avoid a relapse in many cases. A psychotherapist or rehabilitation specialist may assist the patient with developing and rehearsing a plan of action in case an unpleasant or unsettling event occurs. Such a plan might include walking away from situations the schizophrenic finds stressful, telephoning a trusted friend, family member, or doctor to talk about whatever has arisen, or seeking solace in a favorite location such as a peaceful park.

Doctors encourage schizophrenics to participate in physical exercise daily—going on a hike for example—as one way to live successfully with the disease.

Doctors emphasize that eating a healthy diet and getting some daily exercise are other important elements of living successfully with the disease. Although poor nutrition does not actually cause schizophrenia, nutritious food and regular exercise strengthen the body, help the individual withstand infectious diseases like colds and flu, and help prevent serious physical illnesses like heart disease. Family members can play an important role in providing or helping the schizophrenic to cook well-balanced meals and encouraging the person to engage in some sort of enjoyable daily exercise.

Finally, experts advise families to urge their schizophrenic loved one to develop hobbies like painting, gardening, or playing a musical instrument. These types of activities help patients to function better because they give structure and meaning to their days, just like having a job or volunteering to help others gives them a reason to get out of bed in the morning.

Stigma and Schizophrenia

Even when they are able to develop healthy coping skills and engage in productive activities, schizophrenics and their families say one of the most frustrating parts of living with the disease is the stigma attached to this and other severe mental illnesses. One schizophrenic man expressed this very well when he said, "most of the people out there won't come near me or they spit me in the eye . . . they treat most of us like that . . . they are either afraid or hate us . . . I've seen it a thousand times . . . I don't belong . . . they know it and I know it."[37]

Schizophrenics who might otherwise be able to work find that prejudice often confronts them when they look for jobs. Faced with such discrimination, some resort to deception—sometimes with the aid of their doctor. One patient named Maurizio described how his psychiatrist used the words "emotional illness" rather than "schizophrenia" to explain Maurizio's condition in a letter to the dean of the law school Maurizio attended. The doctor feared that Maurizio would never be allowed to practice law if authorities at his school knew he had schizophrenia. Recent enforcement of laws protecting people with disabilities from discrimination in employment has helped some schizophrenics find jobs, but for those whose efforts are stymied by prejudice, it is still difficult, expensive, and time-consuming to prove that such discrimination has occurred.

Another serious consequence of the stigma attached to mental illness is the incidence of violence against schizophrenics. Experts claim that many instances of such violence are not reported because law enforcement officers dismiss schizophrenics' complaints as delusional rantings. But mental health groups reveal that violence, especially against homeless schizophrenics, is not unusual.

Advocacy for the Mentally Ill

Advocacy groups like the National Alliance for the Mentally Ill and Schizophrenics Anonymous have made it a priority to diminish some of the stigma and acts of violence against mentally ill persons by lobbying government officials to enact and enforce protective laws and by educating the public. They offer extensive on-line information, books, pamphlets, periodicals, films, and other media resources to individuals and organizations who request them. In addition, these groups sponsor public seminars and special mental health education campaigns to help achieve their goals. They also endorse efforts by other groups to broaden social acceptance of the mentally ill. One such group, the international Compeer Program, pairs healthy volunteers with mentally ill people for social outings and companionship on a weekly basis in order to diminish the barriers between these individuals. The Compeer participants share mutually enjoyable activities like sports, shopping, going to a movie, or just chatting over a cup of coffee. Sometimes the volunteers and mentally ill individuals are in a similar age group; in other cases adults volunteer to be a friend to a child or vice versa.

These programs have begun to make a difference in how the public perceives people with schizophrenia, but mental health authorities admit there is still much work to be done before the stigma of the disease is no longer a daily obstacle in a schizophrenic's life. Janice, a paranoid schizophrenic, expresses the hope of many living with the disease when she says, "We need to know that we, too, can be active participants in society. We do have something to contribute to this world, if we are only given the opportunity."[38]

Chapter 5

Future Directions

ALTHOUGH SCHIZOPHRENICS TODAY have more of an opportunity to lead productive and satisfying lives than ever before, experts realize there are still many improvements to be made in all aspects of diagnosis and treatment. A recent study at the National Institute of Mental Health, for example, showed that fewer than half of all schizophrenic patients in the United States are currently receiving appropriate treatment for the disease. Mental health professionals and advocacy groups are attempting to increase this percentage and improve future schizophrenia care with several strategies.

One reason that many people do not participate in available treatment programs is denial of the disease by both patients and their families. Mental health groups are therefore escalating their efforts to promote education about symptoms and effective therapies so people will be more likely to recognize the need for treatment. Support groups that offer advice and understanding are also expanding their outreach to convince individuals and families that action, rather than denial, is the most productive approach.

Sometimes people do not participate in therapy programs because they are unaware that such programs exist. Increased public exposure to what is available in certain locations is, accordingly, another major goal of advocacy and support groups, which are also working on establishing treatment facilities in locations where these are not already present.

The Bottom Line

Another reason many schizophrenics are not currently receiving appropriate care is funding. Psychiatrist Herbert Y. Meltzer, past president of the American Psychiatric Association, states,

For patients with schizophrenia, their families, and mental health professionals committed to treating and investigating this group of disorders, now is both the best and worst of times. On the positive side are the development of a new generation of antipsychotic drugs with greater tolerability and efficacy. . . . On the negative side are the control of mental health policy for the treatment of schizophrenia in many of our states and localities by individuals whose decisions are too often driven by fiscal [money] issues.[39]

Other experts agree that many schizophrenics are not getting needed care because oftentimes government programs and medical insurance plans base their treatment decisions on what is cheapest rather than on what is best for individual patients. One area where this is a concern relates to new atypical antipsychotic medicines, which are much costlier than conventional antipsychotics. Many insurance companies and government assistance plans will not pay the extra money, even if the more expensive medicine best suits the needs of a particular patient, meaning that many patients are not getting the best treatment possible. Mental health advocacy groups have future plans to lobby, educate, and promote research in an effort to convince insurers and the federal government to provide funding that will enable all patients to get the medications they need.

Future Goals for Psychotherapy and Rehabilitation

Along with making a complete range of therapy available to schizophrenics from all walks of life, the American Psychiatric Association recognizes the need to improve existing treatment programs. One way doctors are looking to improve treatment strategies is by conducting more scientific research to find out what really works. In the areas of psychotherapy and rehabilitation, for example, scientists are beginning research to answer questions about which sequences of treatment benefit patients most. Studies are focusing on whether it is best for a doctor to prescribe social skills, living skills, or thinking skills therapy first and whether these types of therapy should be given sequentially or simultaneously. Researchers hope that studies that measure various peoples' progress with different sequences will give doctors guidance in designing individual therapy plans. At the present time, most physicians make these decisions based on ex-

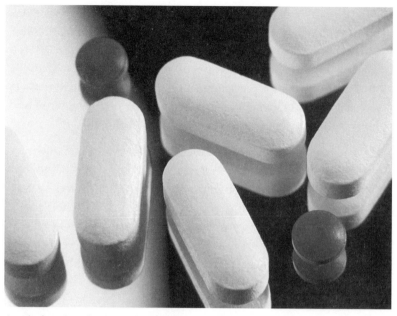

Atypical antipsychotic medications are costly and many times not covered by insurance companies or government agencies.

perience. This may be helpful and effective in many cases, but experts believe that scientific data will supplement individual judgment to help doctors provide more powerful and accurate treatment strategies.

Another area where researchers hope scientific evidence will supplement physicians' experience and intuition is in evaluating the violence potential of psychotic patients. Developing precise assessment guidelines would be invaluable in helping doctors and law enforcement personnel make decisions about who should be forcibly committed to a hospital or jail to protect family members and the public.

The Human Factor

Other research related to human and social elements in therapy is examining how individual psychiatrists and other mental health care professionals influence a patients' recovery. Scientists at the McLean Hospital at Harvard University, for example, are studying how the attitude and behavior of mental health caretakers affects treatment success. Until now such variables have not been scientifically documented, although schizophrenics and their families are no doubt aware of their importance. Many patients have stated that an unusually supportive doctor or staff member was a critical factor in helping them recover. One case involving a catatonic woman illustrates how small gestures by hospital staff members helped the patient climb out of a condition that left her mute and motionless for weeks on end. The woman explains:

> The journey back started in a hospital. There was a nurse who brought me a sweater one time when I had run away without mine. There was a doctor into whose office I was led each week. He sat there beside me in a silence that matched my own. Before words were exchanged between us he would take my hands in his and try to get me to move. What patience he must have had. They did not give up on me. Finally, I began to respond to them.[40]

Directions in Biological Research

In addition to improving schizophrenia care, worldwide efforts are focused on gaining more understanding of the biological factors involved in the disease. This includes research into prevention, diagnosis, causes, and treatments.

A great deal of research is being conducted on the possibility of preventing schizophrenia in individuals with a family history of the disease. Research at the National Institute of Mental Health and other centers is trying to locate the genes that make people susceptible to schizophrenia. Researchers hope that once these genes are identified, it might someday be possible for doctors to alter or replace faulty genes with normal ones, thereby preventing the disease in the first place.

Scientists believe they are getting close to finding some of the genes involved in schizophrenia. One team of researchers at the University of Washington, for example, is studying a gene they refer to as Disheveled-1 that is related to brain development, social interaction, and the filtering of sensory information. They think Disheveled-1 is very likely to play a role in schizophrenia, perhaps by altering brain structures that govern the ability to screen incoming sensations and form social relationships. Other researchers are busy mapping a variety of different genes to determine which ones influence diverse components of the disease.

Related research centers on examining families of people with schizophrenia to find information on how the symptoms are first triggered. A team at Johns Hopkins University's Psychiatric Neuro-Imaging Center, for example, has discovered that mentally healthy relatives of schizophrenics often have brain abnormalities associated with schizophrenia. The scientists are trying to determine exactly why these individuals have not developed the disease even though they possess brain abnormalities that could cause it. These findings could lead to strategies for preventing such abnormalities from progressing to actual cases of schizophrenia.

Scientists believe they are getting close to identifying some of the genes involved in schizophrenia.

Discoveries about other conditions in the body that trigger schizophrenia may also lead to preventive strategies. One line of research is looking at methods of preventing hormones from altering neurons in adolescents with a genetic predisposition toward schizophrenia. Other scientists are trying to determine exactly which viruses might be involved in schizophrenia in hopes that someday high-risk individuals can receive vaccinations against those pathogens. A recent study at the Johns Hopkins School of Medicine, for example, found bits of genetic material from a retrovirus in the cerebrospinal fluid of a group of newly diagnosed schizophrenics. "At this point, whether the virus is causing some of the cases of schizophrenia or whether it's activated during the process, we don't actually know,"[41] says the lead researcher in the project. The investigators believe that if they can prove a link between the virus and the development of the disease,

In the future, doctors hope to develop a blood test that will help diagnose schizophrenia.

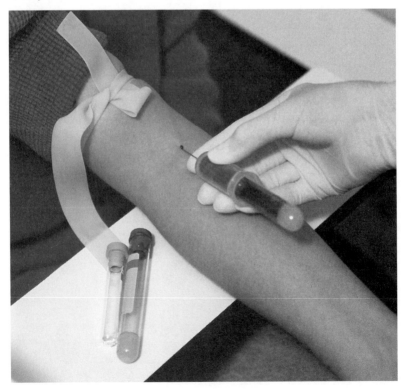

in the future they can work on protecting genetically susceptible people with medicines that destroy that particular virus.

Still other studies like one called the Prevention Research Initiative at the National Institute of Mental Health are trying to pinpoint how and why schizophrenia strikes certain people at various stages of life. One question scientists are trying to answer is why the disease does not become active until age forty or fifty in some people. Researchers are looking into whether there are protective factors such as brain chemistry, immunity to certain viruses, or environmental factors that delay the onset. This research could lead to preventive medications or other strategies to keep symptoms from ever beginning.

Improving Diagnosis

Another important avenue of research centers on improving diagnosis. Right now diagnosis depends on a doctor's assessment of whether a person's symptoms match accepted criteria for schizophrenia. In the future, doctors hope to develop more objective tests. These might include blood tests or brain scans to search for key markers of schizophrenia. At this time no one has discovered chemicals in the blood or brain abnormalities that are always present in schizophrenics. Doctors hope to find qualities or combinations of qualities that are consistently present in order to use these measurements as reliable diagnostic tools. Such tools would speed diagnosis, thereby enabling doctors to begin treatment sooner.

Two good examples of research into diagnosis are projects at the National Institute of Mental Health and at Johns Hopkins University. In one study at the National Institute of Mental Health, researchers are using brain imaging techniques to learn whether abnormal neurons detected in fetuses can be used as reliable predictors of schizophrenia. The scientists plan to track these children to see if they eventually develop the disorder.

At Johns Hopkins University, scientists recently found that many schizophrenics have higher than normal levels of an enzyme called reverse transcriptinase in the cerebrospinal fluid that surrounds the brain and spinal cord. They hope reliable tests for this enzyme can be developed to help in accurately diagnosing schizophrenia. In addition, the researchers believe that such tests could be of use in fine-tuning treatments for the disease. "If you have a marker where you can say, 'if this goes up they are going to have a psychotic episode,' then you might use a slightly different mix of drugs to treat them,"[42] says Dr. Franco Yee, a scientist associated with the project.

Other research centers on developing methods of assessing subtle symptoms that may appear many years before a person actually develops schizophrenia. Many studies find that oftentimes this prodromal period begins very early in a child's life, but at the time no one recognizes that the symptoms have anything to do with schizophrenia. Based on interviews with parents of babies and children who are later diagnosed with schizophrenia, Dr. E. Fuller Torrey and his colleagues at the National Institute of Mental Health noted that many such babies were slow in developing speech and motor skills, were socially withdrawn, and had difficulties being toilet trained. Often as children these individuals were shy, easily upset and hostile when provoked, had difficulties learning in school, had poor coordination, and showed various neurotic quirks like a fear of stairs or an obsession to keep washing their hands.

While many babies and children who display similar behaviors never develop schizophrenia, researchers are hoping to refine methods of determining when and how these traits are likely to signal a tendency to later become schizophrenic. In the future, further knowledge about early symptoms may result in ways of treating these symptoms before they progress to full-blown schizophrenia.

Understanding the Causes of Schizophrenia

Ongoing research on the root causes of schizophrenia can also provide new insight into better diagnostic and treatment methods. Investigators are making huge strides in this direction thanks to modern imaging techniques such as MRI, CT, and PET scans.

In one line of research, doctors at Johns Hopkins University Psychiatric Neuro-Imaging Center are using a newly developed MRI technique known as Fiber Assignment by Continuous Tracking to study abnormal connections between certain areas of the brain in schizophrenics. This technique allows the scientists to accurately trace how nerve fibers from one region of the brain connect to other areas. The researchers explain:

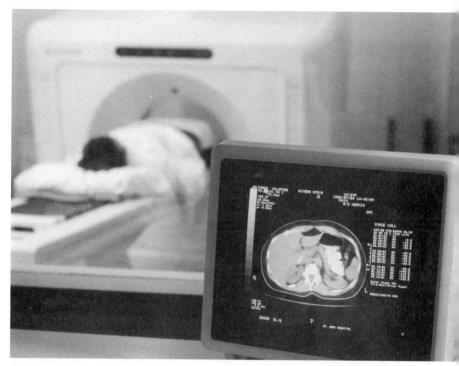

Some researchers are using MRI to show brain abnormalities in schizophrenic patients.

There is strong evidence that brain cortex circuits in people with schizophrenia are "mis-wired" or that normal connections are disrupted. We have developed state-of-the-art software methods for MRI display and measurement of many brain regions, including complex, evolutionarily advanced cortical areas that seem disproportionately affected in people with schizophrenia.[43]

The knowledge gained through such studies could eventually help doctors diagnose and treat the disease by examining and perhaps someday correcting the "mis-wired" brain connections.

Other researchers at Johns Hopkins are using MRI to find out how brain abnormalities produce the disordered language seen in schizophrenia. These investigators are looking at the neuron activity in Wernicke's area, a region of the brain associated with language, in both mentally healthy and schizophrenic people to compare how the neurons respond as the individuals make word associations.

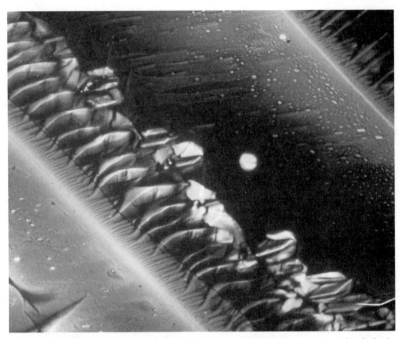

Some studies suggest that the neurotransmitter GABA (shown) may be linked to schizophrenia.

Another group at Johns Hopkins is looking at how physical differences in the brains of men and women might be reflected in differences in the severity and treatability of the disease. Schizophrenic men, for example, are less likely to be helped by antipsychotic medications than schizophrenic women, and these researchers are trying to determine if this has something to do with gender-related variations in the structure and connections in their brains.

At other research centers, doctors are learning more about how specific brain regions control symptoms and behavior. The goal of these diverse projects is to someday develop effective medicines that target specific areas of the brain. Researchers at Washington University in St. Louis, for example, are tracing how brain structures called the prefrontal cortex and anterior cingulate cortex are involved in schizophrenics' disordered thoughts and actions. Studies at the VA Medical Center in Brockton, Massachusetts, are focusing on the loss of brain tissue in areas related to schizophrenia. At Westmead Hospital in Westmead, Australia, scientists are comparing how the amygdala in the brains of normal people and schizophrenics responds to images of threatening and nonthreatening facial expressions. They believe any abnormal responses in schizophrenic brains may be related to symptoms like paranoia.

New knowledge about the role of certain neurotransmitters is also helping doctors gain an understanding of the causes of schizophrenia. Researchers at Columbia University College of Physicians and Surgeons are studying what causes the excess dopamine found in the brains of people with schizophrenia. They are finding that other factors besides too many dopamine receptors are involved, since preliminary results suggest that having too few neurons that use the neurotransmitter glutamate may be the real culprit. This finding is consistent with other researchers' observations that certain illegal drugs, such as angel dust (PCP), which cause the release of glutamate, can produce schizophrenia-like symptoms. Further studies are being set up to determine the exact role this neurotransmitter plays.

Recent studies suggest that the neurotransmitter GABA (garaminobenzoic acid) is also involved in schizophrenia. This chemical is known to play a significant role in allowing the brain to process information in an orderly fashion. Researchers at the University of Newcastle in Australia recently discovered abnormal GABA receptors in the brains of schizophrenics. They are hoping that this and similar research into other neurotransmitters will eventually lead to more effective drug treatments for the disease.

Drugs for the Future

Many new drugs are currently being tested in hopes that patients who are not helped by available drugs will someday find relief from the symptoms of schizophrenia. One drug under investigation at Yale University is called LY354740. It blocks the release of the neurotransmitter glutamate, and investigators hope it might help schizophrenics who do not respond favorably to existing medications that target the neurotransmitter dopamine.

At McLean Hospital, doctors are studying whether a drug already on the market to treat symptoms of Parkinson's disease, selegiline, is useful in treating negative symptoms of schizophrenia. This is important research because most current antipsychotic drugs do not help negative symptoms.

Other efforts center on ways of making existing medications more effective by reducing side effects or improving the way the most effective dose of a drug is determined. Oftentimes, simply taking less of a medication will reduce unpleasant side effects, so finding the minimum effective dose for a particular patient can be very important in determining whether or not the person will continue to take the drug.

Another line of research is attempting to develop long-acting forms of the atypical antipsychotics. There are presently long-acting versions of many conventional antipsychotics, but so far there are none for these newer drugs. Since getting many schizophrenics to consistently take their medication is a problem, longer-acting drugs would help by reducing the number of times the person has to take the drug.

Other Future Treatments

In addition to developing new drugs, researchers are exploring entirely new methods of treating schizophrenia. One experimental treatment being studied at Yale University School of Medicine is called repetitive transcranial magnetic stimulation (rTMS). The technique involves stimulating certain areas in the brain with strong magnets. This treatment decreases the activity of the neurons in these areas. The doctors performing this research are hoping this method will reduce symptoms of schizophrenia in patients who are not helped by antipsychotic medicines.

In one study the Yale research team, led by Ralph Hoffman, M.D., delivered rTMS to an area of the brain known to be involved when schizophrenics hear voices. Each patient received forty minutes of rTMS for four days. Some patients received fake stimulation in the same area during the control phase of the experiment. This way the researchers could determine if the rTMS was really producing any therapeutic effects.

About 75 percent of the patients treated with rTMS reported that the voices disappeared or were heard less often. These effects lasted for several months, even after treatment was stopped. The scientists plan to do further studies to test whether rTMS is a reliable and practical method of reducing such auditory hallucinations in other patients. "If that replicates in a large group of patients . . . we think it would be very promising as a potential clinical tool,"[44] says Hoffman.

More work has to be done before rTMS can be used routinely for these and other symptoms. The researchers need to understand how and why rTMS works, for example. They must also determine its long-term safety and effectiveness.

Can Schizophrenia Be Cured?

The more scientists learn about effective new treatments and underlying causes of schizophrenia, the more they hope that someday they will develop a cure for the disease. Perhaps someday a technique like rTMS

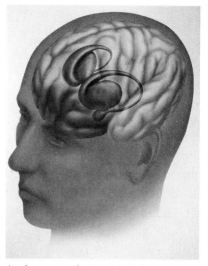

As doctors and researchers learn more about the schizophrenic mind, the more hope they have of developing a cure.

will be fine-tuned to permanently correct the abnormal brain activities that cause hallucinations and other symptoms. Or maybe doctors will prove that neurotransmitter imbalances are definitely responsible for symptoms of the disease and will find a drug that permanently fixes these imbalances.

With all the recent advances in diagnostic technology and understanding of the disease itself, the hope that schizophrenia will someday be conquered seems more and more realistic.

Notes

Introduction: A Terrifying Disease
1. Janice Jordan, "Schizophrenia—Adrift in an Anchorless Reality," *Schizophrenia Bulletin*, vol. 21, no. 23, 1995, p. 1. www.mentalhealth. com/story/p32-SC03.html.
2. Interview with Janice Holmes, family advocate at Transitions Mental Health, San Luis Obispo, CA, March 7, 2001.

Chapter 1: What Is Schizophrenia?
3. Quoted in *Internet Mental Health*, "Our Lives with Schizophrenia," p. 4. www.mentalhealth.com/books/scz/scz-03.html.
4. Eugen Bleuler, *Dementia Praecox or the Group of Schizophrenias* (1911). Trans. Joseph Zinkin. Madison, CT: International Universities Press, 1950, p. 9.
5. Quoted in *Pine Rest Today Magazine*, "Schizophrenia: The Lonely Disease, the Fearful Disease," p. 2. www.pinerest.org/library/todays/prtschiz.htm.
6. Quoted in The University of Texas, "Types of Schizophrenia." p. 2. www.homepage.psy.utexas.edu/homepage/Class/Psy301/Keough/ClassNotes/april28.html.
7. Vicki Ritts, Ph.D., "Infusing Culture into Psychopathology." www.sticc.cc.mo.us/mc/users/vritts/psypath.htm.
8. Ritts, "Infusing Culture into Psychopathology."
9. Ritts, "Infusing Culture into Psychopathology."
10. Quoted in Edward Shorter, *A History of Psychiatry*. New York: John Wiley & Sons, 1997, p. 276.

Chapter 2: What Causes Schizophrenia?
11. Quoted in Shorter, *A History of Psychiatry*, p. 177.
12. National Institute of Mental Health, "Schizophrenia Research at

the National Institute of Mental Health." www.nimh.gov/publicat/schizresfact.htm.

13. Quoted in About.com Neurosciences, "Study Links Abnormal Structure of Brain Region with Greater Intensity of Schizophrenia in Men than Women," p. 2. http://neuroscience.about.com/education/neuroscience/library/pr/blpr000301b.htm.

14. Quoted in *Psychiatric News*, "Schizophrenia Has Origins in Childhood, Says British Expert," March 19, 1999, p. 2.

15. E. Fuller Torrey, and Robert H. Yolken, "Could Schizophrenia Be a Viral Zoonosis Transmitted from House Cats?" p. 2. www.stanleylab.org/Document/zoonosis.html.

16. American Psychiatric Association, "Schizophrenia," p. 6. www.psych.org/psych/htdocs/public_info/schizo.htm.

17. Quoted in About.com Neurosciences, "Study Links Abnormal Structure of Brain Region," p. 2.

Chapter 3: Treatment but No Cure

18. American Psychiatric Association, "APA Online Clinical Resources." p. 4. www.psych.org/psych/htdocs/clin_respg_schizo1.html.

19. Shorter, *A History of Psychiatry*, p. 255.

20. Quoted in Irving Gottesman, *Schizophrenia Genesis*. New York: W. H. Freeman, 1991, p. 41.

21. Quoted in Gottesman, *Schizophrenia Genesis*, p. 42.

22. Susan Baur, *The Dinosaur Man*. New York: Edward Burlingame Books, 1991, p. 2.

23. Baur, *The Dinosaur Man*, p. 3.

Chapter 4: Living with Schizophrenia

24. American Psychiatric Association, "Violence and Mental Illness," January 1998, p. 3.

25. *Internet Mental Health*, "Schizophrenia Important Research (1997–99)," p. 4. www.mentalhealth.com/dis-rs5/p29-ps1d.html.

26. Quoted in *Psychiatric News*, "SA's Successful Formula Uses Peer Groups to Aid Recovery," September 15, 2000, p. 2.

27. Friendship Network, "The Friendship Network Home Page." www.friendshipnetwork.org/index.html.

28. Baur, *The Dinosaur Man*, p. 5.

29. E. Fuller Torrey, *Surviving Schizophrenia*. New York: HarperPerennial, 1995, p. 5.
30. Treatment Advocacy Center, "Episodes Database," 49 of 155 records. www.psychlaws.org/ep.asp.
31. Interview, Janice Holmes.
32. Torrey, *Surviving Schizophrenia*, p. 286.
33. Quoted in Torrey, *Surviving Schizophrenia*, p. 35.
34. Quoted in *Internet Mental Health*, "Our Lives with Schizophrenia." p. 7.
35. National Institute of Mental Health, "Schizophrenia." www.nimh. nih.gov/publicat/schizoph.htm.
36. Quoted in Mental Wellness.com, "Support Groups Empower Family Members," p. 1. www.mentalwellness.com/helphope/ hopeq2.htm.
37. Quoted in Torrey, *Surviving Schizophrenia*, p. 235.
38. Jordan, "Schizophrenia," p. 3.

Chapter 5: Future Directions

39. Herbert Y. Meltzer, American Psychiatric Association, "Treating Schizophrenia in the Millenium," p. 1. www.psych.org/psych/ htdocs/pnews/98-10-02/meltzer.html.
40. Quoted in *Pine Rest Today Magazine*, "Schizophrenia: The Lonely Disease," p. 3.
41. Quoted in Latelinenews.com, "Virus May Contribute to Some Schizophrenia Cases," p. 1. http://latelinenews.com/ll/english/ 1064381.shtml.
42. Quoted in About.com Neurosciences, "Chemical Marker May Help to Diagnose Schizophrenia," p. 2. http://neuroscience.about. com/education/neuroscience/library/pr/blpr991202c.htm.
43. Quoted in Division of Psychiatric Neuro-Imaging at Johns Hopkins University, "Schizophrenia Research at PNI," p. 1. http://pni.med.jhu.edu/Projects_Methods/Mental_Disorders/ schizophrenia2.htm.
44. Quoted in *Psychiatric News*, "Treatment May Reduce Auditory Hallucinations," June 2, 2000, p. 2.

Glossary

antipsychotics: Drugs that are effective in treating psychotic illnesses.

catatonic subtype: A type of schizophrenia where the predominant symptom is staying in a fixed position.

delusions: False beliefs that have no basis in reality.

disorganized subtype: A type of schizophrenia where the primary symptoms are disorganized speech and behavior.

dopamine: A chemical called a neurotransmitter suspected of being involved in schizophrenia.

electroconvulsive shock therapy (ECT): A method of causing convulsions with electric shocks to treat schizophrenia.

gene: The basic unit of hereditary information.

hallucinations: Sensations that aren't really there.

lobotomy: A surgical procedure where a portion of the brain is cut out in order to treat mental illness.

loose associations: Incoherent patterns of thoughts and speech typical in schizophrenia.

neuron: Nerve cell.

neurotransmitters: Chemicals that transmit nerve impulses from one neuron to another.

paranoid subtype: A type of schizophrenia where the person is obsessed that someone or something is out to harm them.

psychiatrist: A medical doctor who specializes in treating mental illness.

psychosis: A severe form of mental illness where the patient cannot distinguish reality from fantasy.

residual subtype: A type of schizophrenia where the person shows mostly negative symptoms.

schizophrenia: A severe medical illness of the brain that affects 1 percent of the population.

undifferentiated subtype: A type of schizophrenia where none of the other subtypes fits the patient.

Organizations to Contact

American Psychiatric Association (APA)
1400 K St. NW
Washington, DC 20005
(888) 357-7924
fax: (202) 682-6850
Internet: www.psych.org

APA offers general information about topics related to mental health, including schizophrenia news, research, and physician referrals.

National Alliance for the Mentally Ill (NAMI)
Colonial Place Three
2107 Wilson Blvd., Suite 300
Arlington, VA 22201–3042
NAMI Helpline: (800) 950-NAMI
(703) 524-7600
fax: (703) 524-9094
TDD: (703) 516-7227
Internet: www.nami.org

NAMI offers information and support for patients, families, and others seeking knowledge about mental illness through its local, state, and national affiliates.

National Institute of Mental Health (NIMH)
Office of Communications and Public Liaison, NIMH Information Resources and Inquiries Branch
6001 Executive Blvd., Room 8184, MSC 9663
Bethesda, MD 20892–9663
(301) 443-4513

fax: (301) 443-4279
Internet: www.nimh.gov

NIMH promotes education and distributes research reports and publications on mental illness.

National Mental Health Association (NMHA)
1021 Prince St.
Alexandria, VA 22314-2971
(703) 684-7722
fax: (703) 684-5968
Mental Health Information Center (800) 433-5959
Internet: www.nmha.org

NMHA gives information and support on a wide range of mental health topics, including schizophrenia.

Schizophrenics Anonymous
Schizophrenics Association Headquarters
403 Seymour Street, Suite 202
Lansing, MI 48933
(800) 482-9534, in Michigan (248) 557-6777
Internet: www.sanonymous.org

Schizophrenics Anonymous is run by patients for patients who share similar struggles and want peer support in their recovery.

For Further Reading

Books

Michelle Friedman, *Everything You Need to Know About Schizophrenia.* New York: Rosen, Need To Know Library, 2000. How schizophrenia can affect a teen's life.

Dan Harmon, *Schizophrenia: Losing Touch with Reality.* Broomall, PA: Chelsea House, 1999. How schizophrenia affects individuals and society.

Peter Wyden, *Conquering Schizophrenia: A Father, His Son, & a Medical Breakthrough.* New York: Alfred A. Knopf, 1998. A detailed account of a challenging quest for treatment, written by the father of a young schizophrenic man.

Journals

Schizophrenia Bulletin, a quarterly journal published by the National Institute of Mental Health, covers all aspects of schizophrenia research and treatment.

Pamphlets

Schizophrenia: Questions and Answers. Information Resources and Inquiries Branch, National Institute of Mental Health.

Websites

Internet Mental Health (www.mentalhealth.com). Internet Mental Health provides information on all aspects of many mental disorders, including schizophrenia.

Mental Wellness.com (www.mentalwellness.com). Mental Wellness.com is a comprehensive online resource about schizophrenia, emphasizing personal stories, support groups, and patient care.

Treatment Advocacy Center (www.psychlaws.org). The Treatment Advocacy Center is a nonprofit organization dedicated to overcoming legal and clinical barriers to the treatment of those with severe mental illness.

Works Consulted

Books

Susan Baur, *The Dinosaur Man*. New York: Edward Burlingame Books, 1991. A therapist's enlightening view of the human side of schizophrenia.

Eugen Bleuler, *Dementia Praecox or the Group of Schizophrenias* (1911). Trans. Joseph Zinkin. Madison, CT: International Universities Press, 1950. Highly technical textbook by the doctor who named the disease schizophrenia.

Irving Gottesman, *Schizophrenia Genesis*. New York: W. H. Freeman, 1991. A good overview of the disease, its history, current status, and patient perspectives.

Edward Shorter, *A History of Psychiatry*. New York: John Wiley & Sons, 1997. Detailed history of psychiatry, information on theories, treatments, important people. Covers other diseases besides schizophrenia.

E. Fuller Torrey, *Schizophrenia and Manic Depressive Disorder*. New York: Basic Books, 1994. Covers research on twins who have schizophrenia.

E. Fuller Torrey, *Surviving Schizophrenia*. New York: HarperPerennial, 1995. Complete overview of symptoms, causes, and treatment as well as an in-depth resource for patients and families.

Periodicals

American Psychiatric Association, "Violence and Mental Illness," January 1998.

C. Arango et al., "Neurological Signs and the Heterogenicity of Schizophrenia," *American Journal of Psychiatry*, vol. 157, no. 4, April 2000, pp. 560–65.

R. M. Bilder et al., "Neuropsychology of First-Episode Schizophrenia: Initial Characterization and Clinical Correlates," *American Journal of Psychiatry* vol. 157, no. 4, April 2000, pp. 549–59.

R. F. Deiken et al., "Reduced Concentrations of Thalamic N-acetylaspartate in Male Patients with Schizophrenia," *American Journal of Psychiatry*, vol. 157, no. 4, April 2000, pp. 644–47.

S. Kapur et al., "Relationship Between Dopamine D(2) Occupancy, Clinical Response, and Side Effects: A Double-Blind PET Study of First-Episode Schizophrenia," *American Journal of Psychiatry*, vol. 157, no. 4, April 2000, pp. 514–20.

P. E. Keck et al., "The Efficacy of Atypical Antipsychotics in the Treatment of Depressive Symptoms, Hostility, and Suicidality in Patients with Schizophrenia," *Journal of Clinical Psychiatry*, 61 Suppl. 3, 2000, pp. 4–9.

J. J. Kim et al., "Regional Neural Dysfunction in Chronic Schizophrenia Studied with Positron Emission Tomography," *American Journal of Psychiatry*, vol. 157, no. 4, April 2000, pp. 542–48.

Psychiatric News, "Glutamate Neuron Deficiency May Be at Root of Schizophrenia," July 7, 2000.

Psychiatric News, "SA's Successful Formula Uses Peer Groups to Aid Recovery," September 15, 2000.

Psychiatric News, "Schizophrenia Has Origins in Childhood, Says British Expert," March 19, 1999.

Psychiatric News, "Treatment May Reduce Auditory Hallucinations," June 2, 2000.

K. Radewicz et al., "Increase in HLA-Immuno-Reactive Microglia in Frontal and Temporal Cortex of Chronic Schizophrenics," *Journal of Neuropathology Experimental Neurology*, vol. 59, no. 2, February 2000, pp. 137–50.

G. Rosoklija et al., "Structural Abnormalities of Subicular Dendrites in Subjects with Schizophrenia and Mood Disorders: Preliminary Findings," *Archives General Psychiatry*, vol. 57, no. 4, April 2000, pp. 349–56.

O. Wittekindt et al., "The Human Small Conductance Calcium-Regulated Potassium Channel Gene (hSKCa3) Contains Two CAG Repeats in Exon 1, Is on Chromosome 1q21.3, and Shows a Possible Association with Schizophrenia," *Neurogenetics*, vol. 1, no. 4, August 1998, pp. 259–65.

Interviews

Janice Holmes, family advocate for Transitions Mental Health, San Luis Obispo, CA, March 7, 2001.

Internet Sources

About.com Neurosciences, "Chemical Marker May Help to Diagnose Schizophrenia." http://neuroscience.about.com/education/ neuroscience/library/pr/blpr991202c.htm.

About.com Neurosciences, "Groundbreaking Yale Research on Brain Receptors Could Yield Better Treatments for Schizophrenia and Parkinson's." http://neuroscience.about.com/education/ neuroscience/library/pr/blpr00030/c.htm.

About.com Neurosciences, "Researchers Looking into Origins of Schizophrenia." http://neuroscience.about.com/education/neuroscience/ library/pr/blpr0002241.htm.

About.com Neurosciences, "Schizophrenia Drug Clozapine Linked to Five Deaths." http://neuroscience.about.com/education/neuro- science/library/pr/blpr000330a.htm.

About.com Neurosciences, "Study Links Abnormal Structure of Brain Region with Greater Intensity of Schizophrenia in Men than Women." http://neuroscience.about.com/education/neuroscience/ library/pr/blpr000301b.htm.

American Psychiatric Association, "APA Online Clinical Resources." www.psych.org/psych/htdocs/clin_res/pg_schizo_1.html.

American Psychiatric Association, "Disease Definition, Natural History, and Epidemiology." www.psych.org/psych/htdocs/clin_res/ pg_schizo_2.html.

American Psychiatric Association, "Let's Talk Facts About Schizophrenia." www.psych.org/public_info/PDF/schizo.pdf.

American Psychiatric Association, "Research Directions." www. psych. org/clin_res/pg_schizo_6.clin.

American Psychiatric Association, "Schizophrenia." www.psych.org/ psych/htdocs/public_info/schizo.html.

Athabasca University, "Diagnostic Categories: Types of Schizophrenia—A Self-Instructional Exercise." http://server.bmod.athabascau. ca/html/Psych433/Tutorial/exer.shtml.

Maurizio Baldini, *Internet Mental Health*, "Maurizio Baldini's Story."

www.mentalhealth.com/story/p32-sc01.html.

Brigham Young University, "Abnormal Psychology Schizophrenia." www.byu.edu/~psychweb/bhc/ab/ab-n19.htm.

California State University-Stanislaus, "The Role of Dopamine Receptors in Schizophrenia." www.chem.csustan.edu/chem4400/SJBR/Mann.htm.

Division of Psychiatric Neuro-Imaging at Johns Hopkins University, "Schizophrenia Research at PNI." http://pni.med.jhu.edu/Projects_Methods/Mental_Disorders/schizophrenia2.htm.

Friendship Network, "The Friendship Network Home Page." www.friendshipnetwork.org/index.html.

Internet Mental Health, "Our Lives with Schizophrenia." www.mentalhealth.com/books/scz/scz-03.html.

Internet Mental Health, "Schizophrenia Important Research (1997–99)." www.mentalhealth.com/dis-r5/p29-ps1d.html.

Janice Jordan, "Schizophrenia—Adrift in an Anchorless Reality," *Schizophrenia Bulletin*, vol. 21, no. 3, 1995. www.mentalhealth.com/story/p32-SC03.html.

Latelinenews.com, "Virus May Contribute to Some Schizophrenia Cases." http://latelinenews.com/ll/english/1064381.shtml.

Living with Schizophrenia, "What Happens to Your Relative During a Stay in a Hospital?" www.nsf.org.uk/information/living_with_schiz/09_hospitalstay.html.

McLean Hospital, Harvard University, "Studies in Clinical Psychiatry." www.hmchet.harvard.edu/psych/redbook/13.htm.

Herbert Y. Meltzer, American Psychiatric Association, "Treating Schizophrenia in the Millennium." www.psych.org/psych/htdocs/ pnews/98-10-02/meltzer.html.

Mental Wellness.com, "Support Groups Empower Family Members." www.mentalwellness.com/helphope/hopeq2.htm.

NARSAD Reasearch, "NARSAD-Funded Research on Schizophrenia Conducted over the Last Two Years."www.mnsource.com/narsad/bd/schres_abc.html.

National Institute of Mental Health, "Progressive Brain Changes Detected in Childhood Onset Schizophrenia." www.nimh.gov/events/prschiz.htm.

National Institute of Mental Health, "Schizophrenia." www.nimh.gov/mhsgrpt/chapter4/sec4.html.

National Institute of Mental Health, "Schizophrenia." www.nimh. nih.gov/publicat/schizoph.htm.

National Institute of Mental Health, "Schizophrenia Research at the National Institute of Mental Health." www.nimh.nih.gov/ publicat/schizresfact.htm.

NISAD, "Current Research in Schizophrenia." www.nisad.org. au/sitemap/info/cur_res.html.

Physicians of the Penn State Geisinger Health System, "Schizophrenia." www.psghs.edu.

Pine Rest Today Magazine, "Schizophrenia: The Lonely Disease, the Fearful Disease." www.pinerest.org/library/todays/prtschiz.htm.

Vicki Ritts, Ph.D., "Infusing Culture into Psychopathology." www.sticc.cc.mo.us/mc/users/vritts/psypath.htm.

E. Fuller Torrey, and Robert H. Yolken, "Could Schizophrenia Be a Viral Zoonosis Transmitted from House Cats?" www.stanleylab.org/ Document/zoonosis.html.

Treatment Advocacy Center, "Episodes Database." www.psychlaws. org/ep.asp.

Treatment Advocacy Center, "Schizophrenia Facts." www.psychlaws. org/General%20Resources/Fact5.htm.

University of Florida, "MRI Scans Reveal Subtle Brain Differences in People with Schizophrenia, UF Researchers Find."www.napa.ufl. edu.99news/schizo.htm.

University of Michigan, "Meador-Woodruff Lab: Our Research." http://www.umich.edu/~jmwlab/research.html.

University of Texas, "Types of Schizophrenia." http://homepage.psy. utexas.edu/homepage/Class/Psy301/Keough/ClassNotes/april 28.html.

Robert H. Yolken, and E. Fuller Torrey, "Viruses as Etiological Agents of Schizophrenia." www.stanleylab.org/document/ etiological/ 20agents.html.

blank page

Index

Picture Credits

About the Author

Melissa Abramovitz has been writing books, articles, poetry, and short stories as a freelance writer for children, teenagers, and adults for over fifteen years. She has published hundreds of articles, numerous short stories and poems, one adult novel, and five children's books during this time.

The author grew up in San Diego, California, and graduated summa cum laude with a degree in psychology from the University of California at San Diego in 1976. She currently lives in San Luis Obispo, California, with her husband, two teenage sons, and two dogs who think they are kids.